UNDERGROUND ACT®* SOLUTIONS VOL 1 -TEST FORM 0661C

The unofficial solutions to the official ACT practice test form 0661C

I0165005

By

Rajiv Raju

and

Silpa Raju

Platypus Global Media

Publisher:

Platypus Global Media

Registered with the U.S. ISBN agency

Contact Publisher at: **pgmdirect@gmail.com**

Available from major wholesalers worldwide. Printed at multiple locations worldwide.

ISBN: 978-0-9842212-2-6

The content of this book is not endorsed or approved by the ACT$^{®*}$, Inc.

CONTENTS

Notes

AUTHORS

Rajiv Raju is a recent graduate of Barrington High School (IL). He wrote the Mathematics, Science and Reading sections of this book. He scored perfect 36 composite score on the ACT. He is the author of the bestselling ACT preparation books **Dissecting the ACT** and **DISSECTING THE ACT 2.0**.

Silpa Raju is a student at Barrington High School (IL) at the time of publication. She wrote the English section of this book. She scored a perfect 36 on the English section of the ACT. She is a co-author of the bestselling ACT preparation books **Dissecting the ACT** and **DISSECTING THE ACT 2.0**.

Visit the authors' blog at : **36onACT.com**

INTRODUCTION

Instructions for obtaining the official ACT test form 0661C.
This book is intended to be used in conjunction with the official ACT test form 0661C.The test form 0661C was included in the free booklet called Preparing for the ACT during the 2006/2007, 2007/2008 and 2008/2009 school years. It is no longer officially available from the ACT. However, the pdf file for this version of the booklet can be found at various locations on the internet. Try a Google search for "ACT test form 0661C". Due to copyright restrictions, these questions cannot be reproduced in this book. The authors have setup a website to help you download the pdf file from archived sources:

http://freeacttest.blogspot.com/

For additional help in locating the test form 0661C, contact the authors at:

dissectingact@yahoo.com

Please note that the content of this book in not approved or endorsed by the ACT®*, inc.

Notes

ACT ENGLISH TEST EXPLANATIONS
By **Silpa Raju**

Please refer to the questions in the English component of the practice test in official ACT booklet, <u>Preparing for the ACT</u> (form 0661C).

1) The concept being tested in this question is redundancy. Choice A, or no change, is wrong because "associated" and "connected" are synonyms, and only one is necessary to get the point across. Choice B, "connected by some of them", when put into the sentence, would read like this: "For some people, traditional American Indian music is connected by some of them with high penetrating vocals accompanied by a steady drumbeat". Although this sentence removes the redundancy of the first choice, it introduces a new error. The sentence has already noted the people who link traditional American Indian music with high penetrating vocals and a steady drumbeat, so the "them" in choice B is unnecessary and creates confusion. Choice C does not fix the error of redundancy in the first choice, because "linked" and "association" both mean to join. Choice D, however, removes redundancy by using one word, associated, and does not introduce any other errors. Therefore, **choice D** is the correct answer for this question.

2) This question requires rhetorical skills knowledge. There is no error with the sentence as it is. Choice G is incorrect because of the parenthetical phrase, "one might say". This phrase is irrelevant and unnecessary to the sentence. Choice H is wrong because "really quite popular" is unnecessarily wordy and confusing. Choice J can be eliminated because like the other choices, it contains more superfluous wording. **Choice F**, or no change, is the best choice because the sentence was correct as it was.

3) Question 3 tests punctuation. It asks which of the choices is NOT acceptable. If we look at choice, we see that it contains a

semi-colon, so there is no error because it has eliminated the run on sentence we see in choice B, which separates two independent clauses with a comma. Compound sentences, when joined by a comma, must consist only of dependent clause and a independent clause, where as this sentence tries to combine two independent clauses. Choice C separates the two independent clauses by putting them into their own sentences, thus separating ideas. Choice C, like choice D, avoids the error of a run-on sentence with a semi-colon, which correctly joins the two clauses. **Choice B** is the correct answer because it is creating an error.

4) Here you see a construction error. A construction error is when words are misplaced and they make a different meaning. In the phrase, "music that performed", it seems as though the music performed. To imply that it is a social music performed at weddings, you must get rid of the "that", because none of the choices involve an "is", which is necessary if you have a "that" in the phrase. Choice G is wrong because "music in which it is performed" does not work because the sentence would read: "It is a social music in which it is performed at weddings, birthday parties, and feasts." Here you are saying that the music is performed within itself, which makes no sense whatsoever. In choice H, music, performing, is not a suitable choice because of the –ing ending. You do not need an –ing in the phrase here, and generally, one should avoid –ing. It also sounds like the music is performing itself. **Choice J** is the only logical answer because "music, performed" uses the correct ending, -ed (past tense) and makes the sentence flow well, so it reads- "It is a social music, performed at weddings, birthday parties, and feasts." The commas correctly break the sentence.

5) Comma usage is being tested here. Choice B is not correct because it has too many commas; the use of a comma after "word" is unnecessary, as well as after "itself". Choice C doesn't work because again, the comma after "word" is not needed. Choice D is incorrect because no comma is necessary after "itself". Therefore, **choice A** is the best choice because it uses no unnecessary commas. In fact, it doesn't use any commas, because none are needed.

6) This question tests if you know how to fix the incorrect placement of a modifier. The phrase "Cheek to cheek, the dance is performed to the relaxed two-stepped tempo" is incorrect. The modifier, or the part before the comma (cheek to cheek), is modifying what? Obviously it is not modifying the dance, but the people. The noun being modified should follow after the modifying phrase. So we can eliminate some choices from here- which ones don't have a phrase about persons immediately after the comma? Choice J doesn't, so we can eliminate that. If we look at choice H, we see that the modifying phrase before the comma is totally changed to "a relaxed two-step tempo". We can use our same principle here. What should "a relaxed two-step tempo" modify? The phrase has it modifying the couple, which makes no sense, so choice J is out. The only remaining **choice is G**, where there is no separated modifier, just a phrase, "Couples dance cheek to cheek to the relaxed two-step tempo". There is no error in this phrase, and it is the only remaining choice, so it is correct.

7) Like question 5, this question tests comma usage. If you look at choice B, you see unnecessary commas after "long" and "past", which makes the choice incorrect. Answer C also introduces excess commas, which are unnecessary after "play" and "past". Finally, choice D has an unneeded comma after "play", making it wrong. So, **choice A**, no change, is the correct answer.

8) This question tests whether you know your tenses or not. If we observe choice F, no change, we see that the word "were" is past tense, though the sentence itself is present tense because of "step", which is present tense. So we must find a choice that agrees with the present tense of this sentence. Choice H uses the word "have", which means they have already done it, so that wouldn't work. Choice J uses "will", which is future tense, making it wrong. **Choice G** is the only choice that uses a present tense verb, "are". The word fits the sentence because it is present tense.

9) Plural or singular? There, their, they're, its, or it's? The sentence is asking for a pronoun, so we need to pick the right one. Choice B isn't fit for the sentence because "they're" is an

abbreviation for "they are", and the sentence, "As the dancers step to the music, they are also stepping in time to a sound that embodies their unique history and suggests the influence of outside cultures on their music." would not make any sense. Choice C is singular, and we are looking for a plural pronoun because of the word "dancers", which is plural, so it is wrong. Choice D isn't a word, making it incorrect. The correct **choice is A**, because "their" is singular and is a fit pronoun to replace "dancers".

10) Here we see a rhetorical skills question. The writer of the passage wants to add the sentence "The agricultural practices of the O'odham are similar to those of the Maya.". In context of the passage, the last sentence of the paragraph 2 is "As the dancers step to the music, they are also stepping in time to a sound that embodies their unique history and suggests the influence of outside cultures on the music." The sentence of paragraph 3 says "The O'odham in the 1700s first encountered the guitars of Spanish missionaries." So, would the sentence about agricultural practices fit between those two? Probably not. One sentence is talking about dancing, while the other is talking about missionaries from Spain. So, armed with the knowledge that it doesn't fit, we can already eliminate choices F and G, because they state that it does fit. Look at choice H; it says that the sentence shouldn't be there because the author has not mentioned a connection between the Mayas and the O'odham. However, the author did mention that outside groups influence culture, so if he had said that the Mayas contributed to the culture surrounding waila, then it might have worked. However, to throw in a sentence about agriculture when you are talking about music and dancing is random, and distracts from the point. **Choice J** states just that, therefore making it correct.

11) This is a construction problem. If we look at the question, we see it asks which placement of the phrase would be wrong. Choice A, where it is, works because when we read the sentence as it is, it makes sense. Choice B is also correct, because it would read "In the 1700s, the O'odham first encountered the guitars of Spanish missionaries." and it follows all of our modification rules. Choice D is also correct because the sentence would say "The O'odham first encountered the guitars of Spanish missionaries in the 1700s."

which makes perfectly good sense. Choice C is wrong because it would be like adding a random phrase into a sentence, which makes it confusing and distracts from the point. Since we are looking for the wrong placement, **Choice C** is the right answer.

12) You will need to know your tenses to solve this one. This sentence is past tense. F is wrong because it unnecessarily uses "have" in front of the borrowed. Watch out for unnecessary "have" usage in sentences. Choice G is present tense, so that wouldn't work with a past tense sentence. Choice H, "were borrowed" is incorrect because it is implying that the O'odham were borrowed, when in fact the sentence is trying to get across the dancing that was borrowed, not the O'odham. **J is the simplest choice, as well as the correct one**. It uses past tense, and is very concise.

13) This is a construction question. They are asking which parenthetical phrases are most relevant to the paragraph. Answer B talks about fiddles being used in waila long ago. Although this may be a tempting choice, considering it has to do with waila, there is a better choice. Choice C says instruments are often made of metal, but does this have anything to do with the paragraph? We want germane information. Choice D says that these instruments are found frequently in jazz bands. This also has no relation to the passage. **Choice A** is the only correct choice because the phrase in the parenthesis, as it is, provides relevant information that aids the reader in understanding why there are saxophones in waila. This is the only information that the reader might need, out of all the choices.

14) In question 14, you are being tested on whether you know where to put punctuation. The sentence is actually fine without punctuation, making **choice G** correct. Choice F is incorrect because no semi-colon is needed there; semi-colons are used to separate two independent clauses, like conjoining two sentences into one. Choice H is also wrong because a colon signifies that a list is coming up. There is no list in this sentence. Choice J is incorrect because a comma is used here, where no pause is needed.

15) Here's another one of those rhetorical skills questions. It's asking which paragraph the sentence they give you would be best to put after. The sentence talks about German influences, so we need to find where they say anything about Germans. It appears that paragraph 3's last sentence says that the Germans' music influenced waila. Paragraph 3's last sentence is the only place where they even say anything about Germans, making it the correct paragraph to put the sentence after. Therefore, **choice C**, paragraph 3, is the right answer.

16) This question does not test your grammar, like most questions on the ACT English Test. Instead, it tests your word choices. Which of the words fits best? Choice A, no change, wouldn't work very well because the difference between Korean years and American years is not a competition. G, or change, is also incorrect because, like contest, the Korean and American ways are different, not a change. H is also incorrect because a dispute is more of a fight, and this year-difference isn't a fight at all. **Choice J** is the correct answer because it uses the word "difference" in the sentence, which is exactly what Korean years and American years are like; different.

17) This question is testing if you know how to make parenthetical phrases. Choice A is incorrect because since there is a comma after "system", but this is meant to set off a phrase. In order to set off a phrase, you must have two commas, one at the beginning of the phrase and one at the end. C is also wrong because a colon signifies that a list is coming, and there is no list in the sentence. Finally, choice D is incorrect because "a person who, according ..." wouldn't make any sense. A person who what? **Choice B** is the best answer because it uses a comma after "person" to complete the parenthetical phrasing by adding the starting comma.

18) This is a rhetorical skills question. This sentence really doesn't fit in the paragraph- We are talking about how the birthday system in Korea works, not about birthdays worldwide. We can eliminate choice F. Let's eliminate the other irrelevant choices. Choice G is also wrong because again, it is off topic and does not fit into the paragraph. Choice H is also wrong for the same reason as the other choices. Only **choice J** works, because it

deletes the unnecessary sentence all together, making the paragraph stay on topic.

19) Here, we must pick the word that correctly describes the "celebration" the author speaks of. "Heightened" could mean lifted, but in this case, it means "to show light upon". This would be an acceptable word for the sentence, making choice A correct. Choice B is incorrect because "raised", when put in this sentence, would mean literally lifted up. If you said something like "raised importance" or "raised awareness" that would make more sense. Choice C is also incorrect because "lifted" means to physically pick something up. Choice D is wrong because "lighted" wouldn't make sense in the sentence- instead you would have to say "shed light upon". **Choice A** is the best answer.

20) We must identify what the passage would lose if the author were to delete the preceding sentence. Choice G is incorrect because the sentence doesn't talk literally about what happens at birthdays, it's just talking about what New Year's could be thought of. Choice H is also wrong because the sentence isn't defending anything, and there is no case in the passage; the passage is simply comparing the American system of birthday counting to that of the Korean system, not trying to choose which is better. Choice J is incorrect because the sentence isn't actually talking about the Korean counting system at all- once again, it is talking about the importance of New Year's Day and the celebration. Notice how all of the choices, except choice F, are incorrect because they don't relate to the sentence the question is referring to. **Choice F** is the best answer because it talks about the "significance" of the celebration, which is exactly what the sentence is talking about.

21) Question 21 is similar to question 19- they both ask you to choose the right word. The sentence needs a word or words that support a point. Choice A, otherwise, would be used to compare two things. Answer B is also used to compare things; though this, that. Choice D is used to talk about something in the past. None of these help to support a point, so **C is the best answer** because "in fact" is adding another significant

point to the argument.

22) Idiom-usage is being tested here. Choice G is wrong because "on" means "above" or "upon", so that wouldn't make much sense with "point". Choice H is also wrong because "at" is the wrong preposition- "point to" is the better preposition. Choice J, or deleting the preposition all together, would disrupt the sentence's flow by removing an essential preposition. **Answer F** is the only correct choice because "point to" uses the correct preposition. Remember that idioms are solid rules that you have to follow- you cannot explain why "at" is the wrong preposition and "to" isn't, for it is just an idiom-usage rule.

23) This question tests punctuation and plurality. Choice B is incorrect because the word "a" is talking about one person and the noun "persons" is plural. Choice C is also wrong because, again, "persons" is plural, and "a" is singular. Choice D is wrong, not because of plurality, but because it introduces another error. It adds an unnecessary comma after the phrase "person's age" and no pause in the sentence is needed there. The only acceptable **choice is A**, because person's age is singular and has no other punctuation errors.

24) Here we are tested on pronoun usage. In order to use a pronoun in a sentence, it must be referring to someone or something. In this sentence, who is "their" referring to? This makes choice F incorrect, because we do not know who "their" is. Choice G is also incorrect because "one's" idea could mean anyone. Choice H is wrong because "it's" is referring to an object or creature. This sentence is not in need of a pronoun, because it does not refer to anyone or anything in particular. **Choice J** is the only correct answer because "this" is not a pronoun.

25) You should know your idiomatic expressions for this question. It's hard to explain to you why any of the answers are wrong, for idioms have no rules; they are just the way they are. All of the choices except B are the wrong words to make this idiom work. **Choice B** is the best answer.

26) This is a rhetorical skills question. Which choice best implies the elders' positive attitudes towards the practice of adding a

year? Choice G means basically "doing what everyone else does", so that's not the best answer. Choice H is wrong because "living with two birthdays themselves" doesn't really imply any positive connotation. Choice J is also incorrect because "obligingly" means "doing as you're told". **Choice F**, "with great enthusiasm", definitely implies a positive connotation, because of the use of "enthusiasm", which says that the elders enjoy adding a year to their age.

27) This question deals with an idiom as well as unclear pronoun reference. Choice B is not correct because "whose" refers to persons, not things (society). There needs to be a number agreement in the sentence. Choice C is also wrong because "this" is an idiom error. Choice D is incorrect because whom is referring to a person, not a thing (society). **Choice A** is the only correct answer because it uses the correct pronoun and refers to things, not people.

28) Your rhetorical skills are tested in this question. Choice F is incorrect because the sentence the question is referring to doesn't have a personal nor a reflective tone. Choice G is also wrong because the sentence isn't really humorous at all. Choice J is not correct because the writer does not express support for either side, the Korean way of counting or the American way of counting. **Choice H** is the only correct answer because the phrases the question talks about are relevant to show contrast between the young and the old.

29) You'll need to know some basic vocabulary for this question. Here, we want to choose the least repetitive choice. Choice A is incorrect because balk and refuse both mean the same thing, and you wouldn't hesitate if you refused, you would simply not do whatever is being asked. Choice B is also wrong because, like choice A, if you balked, you would not bother to hesitate, but instead refuse completely. Choice C is not correct because refuse and balk both mean the same thing, so you wouldn't have to have both. **Choice D** is the best choice because balk means to refuse, and eliminates repetition, while making sense unlike some of the other choices.

30) Which word would best imply that something is simple, but

could prove to be a little difficult? Choice F is not correct because "visibly simple" means that it is most definitely simple, and does not imply that it could be potentially difficult. You might be tempted to choose this because visibly could mean on the outside, but there are better options. Choice H is incorrect because "entirely" also does not imply that there could perhaps be any difficulty whatsoever. Choice J, "fully" also creates the same error as the other choices. **Choice G** is the word that would fit best into the sentence because "apparently" casts doubt upon whatever is being described, so when we say something is "apparently simple", we are implying that it may look simple, but that might not be the case. "Apparently" casts more doubt than "visibly simple" does.

31) Which of the answers best illustrates "dress code" in the sentence? If we look at the sentence, we see the words "certain types of clothing", so our ideal choice would have a list of certain types of clothing that aren't aloud in this "dress code". With this in mind, we can eliminate all the choices except answer C, which contains a list of clothing describing what the dress code would prohibit. When you give examples, it best supports whatever you are talking about. **Choice C** is the best answer.

32) For this question, you'll need to choose the best words to describe how the students act toward school work. Choice F, inefficient toward, doesn't make much sense- you would probably say inefficient with school work, not inefficient toward school work. Choice G does not keep a serious tone like the rest of the essay, nor does choice H. This makes **choice J** the best choice because it uses a serious tone, while describing just how the children would act toward school work.

33) We need a good introductory sentence for the paragraph. Choice B is probably not a good sentence to start a paragraph because the principal was not mentioned anywhere in the paragraph at all, and it doesn't matter what the principle said; the fact that Kevin Bannister violated the dress code is enough proof as to why he got sent home. Choice C is also a wrong answer because there is no support for the statement- again, the principle is mentioned nowhere in the passage. Choice D

is incorrect because the statement is completely irrelevant. It doesn't matter whether this happened at a bad time or a good time. **Choice A** is the best answer because by leaving the first sentence as it is, you are introducing the paragraph and hinting at what will be in the paragraph. By telling that Kevin and his parents felt that their rights had been violated, you are introducing that they were unhappy with the school, which leads into the lawsuit that follows.

34) Punctuation is being tested in this question. This phrase actually needs no punctuation, so we can eliminate all choices with punctuation, making **H the best answer**. Choice F is wrong because a colon signals that a list will follow, and there is no list in this sentence. Choice G is wrong because by putting a comma after "Court", you are putting in an unnecessary pause. Choice J is also incorrect because there is a comma, which puts in a pause that is not needed.

35) Idiomatic phrases are being used in this sentence. Once again, idioms are special rules that you must memorize. There is no explanation as to why one answer is wrong and the other isn't- its just the idiom's rule. Answer **C is the best choice** because "to" is the correct word to put before "wear". Notice that all verbs can have a "to" before them: to dance, to sing, to fall, to jump, to run. "Wear" is a verb, and therefore can have "to" before it, not for, thus eliminating choice A. Choice B, "of wearing" is incorrect because there is no need for an –ing after wear. Be cautious of –ing words on this test; they are often unnecessary and are there to confuse you. Choice D is wrong because you need to have some sort of transitional word between "right" and "wear".

36) In this question, you must know your comma rules. Choice F is incorrect because "however" needs to be set off by commas, for it is an unnecessary word within the sentence. There is a comma before "however" but not after, so it is wrong. Choice H is wrong because "noted however" is not the unnecessary word in the sentence; in fact, it is a phrase, not a word. Choice J is also incorrect because "however" has one comma after it, and you need two to set off a word/phrase- one before, and one after. **Choice G** is the best choice because it correctly

sets off "however" by adding a comma before and after the word.

37) This question tests rhetorical skills. Edit out what you don't need. Choice A isn't- we don't really need to know that authority figures guided the educational process. Choice B is also off topic because the paragraph has nothing to do about changes from the past. Choice C is incorrect because, well, the added "the process we all know well" just isn't necessary- and who says all of us "know well"? **Choice D** is the best answer because it makes the sentence concise and doesn't add any totally irrelevant phrases at the end.

38) You will need to know about contractions for this question. Choice F is wrong because "it's" is a contraction for "it is". The sentence needs the kind of "it" that implies possession. Choice G is also wrong because "they're" is short for "they are" and again, you need a possessive word, not one that uses "it" or "are" to follow up with a description. Choice J is also wrong because "ones" could mean anyone, not just the board. **Choice H** is the best answer because "its" is the possessive word that is singular, so you can use it on "the board" which is a singular noun.

39) You will see plenty of questions about idioms on the ACT, and here is just one of the many. Choice B is wrong because it uses the wrong word, and it doesn't satisfy the idiom, and so are choices C and D. **Choice A** is the one correct answer because it is the right word for this idiom. Once again, you'll have to memorize these rules of idioms- there are no tricks to figure it out.

40) Here is a rhetorical skills question. Choose the right word that hints at what will happen next. Choice G is wrong because "thus" isn't a good word to use here- you can't set off "thus" with commas. "Thus" must be followed by a verb. H is also wrong because "moreover" implies that there is a bigger reason, but the sentence doesn't announce a bigger reason for the court's decision. Answer J is also wrong because "however" implies that there is something opposite from what is going on. "However" could imply irony, something bad if things are good, something good if things are bad, etc.- pretty

much any opposition. There is no opposition between the court and anyone else in this particular sentence. The answer is **choice J**.

41) We need to use the correct tense and idiom in the sentence. Choice A uses the correct tense by using –ing, but uses the wrong word for the idiom. Choice B is wrong for the same reason. Choice D is using the wrong tense- worn is past tense, and we need a present tense verb. **Choice C** is the best answer because it uses a present tense word and eliminates the unnecessary idiomatic phrase.

42) This is another rhetorical skills question. Pick the choice sentence that shows how important Kevin's case is. Choice G is a reminder to you, not a statement that conveys importance. Choice H is talking mostly about the courts, and not specifically about the case. Choice J is wrong because again, it does not illustrate the importance of the case. **Choice F** is the best answer because it directly states "Kevin Bannister's case was significant", which is what the question asks for.

43) Punctuation is being tested in this question. **C is the best answer** because the phrase does not need any commas, and C is comma-free. All the other choices unnecessarily use commas to create breaks in the sentence, which is not needed.

44) This is an idiom error, where you need to pick the correct preposition. Choice G probably isn't the best answer because on literally means "above" or "on top of", so that wouldn't work. Choice H means "together" so that isn't the best choice either. Choice J means "has to do with" and that wouldn't fit too well with the sentence. The best answer would be **choice F**, because "in" public education implies "in the area of public education", which is exactly what we are looking for.

45) This is another rhetorical skills question. Did the essay try to persuade students to exercise their rights? Not really. Choice A is incorrect because Kevin Bannister didn't actually do anything to persuade other students to make full use of their

rights. Choice B is wrong because the essay only focuses on Kevin, and no other students. Choice C is also incorrect because the essay does not suggest that the right to wear blue jeans wasn't significant. The whole essay is based on the violation of Kevin's right to wear blue jeans, implying that it is quite important. **Choice D** is the best answer because the essay does only talk about one student, Kevin Bannister, and explains his constitutional right that was violated. The essay does not persuade others to make use of all their rights, but instead tells the story of an unfair punishment that violated one's rights.

46) This is a construction question. Choice F doesn't really fit in the blank too well because "since" in the context of this sentence would mean "from then onward", and we aren't talking about what has happened from the past to the future. Choice H is incorrect because "concerning" means "having to do with" and we already know it has something to do with this belief of his. Choice J is just wrong idiom-usage. **Choice G** is the best answer because "because of" implies that because of this belief, he was fooled by these girls.

47) Here's a rhetorical skills question. What would the essay lose if the author deleted the first sentence of the paragraph? Answer B is incorrect because there are no humorous parts of the essay, and the sentence isn't irrelevant. Choice C is wrong because the first sentence does not explain Sir Arthur Conan Doyle's motivations at all- it questions something you may think about him. Choice D is also incorrect because the sentence does not describe any setting. **Choice A** is the correct answer because the sentence does set up a contrast- the first sentence says you may think he is a logical person but the next sentences starts with a "but", introducing a contrast, and then tells how he believed in mythical creatures and fantasy, which are not very logical. The "but" is a very key word here, for it tells the reader that there is a contrast coming.

48) This question also deals with plurality. Answer F is incorrect because "girl's" is singular, while "faces" is plural. Choice H is wrong because it does not have an apostrophe in the word "girls" to show possession, of in this case, a face. Choice J is also incorrect because the apostrophe is placed in the word

"face's" and the girl has possession, not the face. **Choice G** is the best answer because the apostrophe is placed appropriately after "girls", which shows that the girls have possession, while sticking to plurality rules.

49) Try and avoid redundancy here, and be concise. In choice A, "true" and "factual" basically mean the same thing, so that choice is redundant, making it incorrect. In choice B, "evident" and "apparent" are the same, and you don't need the "but" because there is no comparison, making it wrong. Choice C is long and unnecessary. **Choice D** is best because "this apparent" best gets the point across, while hinting at a bit of skepticism and being concise.

50) We need to use the right pronoun here. In choice F, the "however" makes a run on sentence. Choice H is wrong because it refers to an item or object, and choice J is wrong because it makes a run-on. **Answer G is correct** because because "who" refers to people and does not make a run on. This is another rhetorical skills question. Do keep in mind, however, that the shortest answer is not always the best answer. Choice A is incorrect because the answer is extremely long and unnecessarily complicated. The word "being" just sounds weird. D can also be eliminated because of this of an idiom error dealing with "where". Choice B is wrong because "in which the magazine where" does not make sense because the sentence has already acknowledged the fact that the article is in a magazine and is telling location twice unnecessarily. In addition, you do not need to write "in which" and "where" in this phrase twice because they serve the same purpose- to tell where the article was put. **Choice G** is the correct answer because "in which" correctly tells where the article was and is short, introduces no grammatical errors, and does not sound eccentric.

51) This is another rhetorical skills question. Do keep in mind, however, that the shortest answer is not always the best answer. Choice A is incorrect because the answer is extremely long and unnecessarily complicated. The word "being" just sounds weird. D can also be eliminated because of this of an idiom error dealing with "where". Choice B is wrong because

"in which the magazine where" does not make sense because the sentence has already acknowledged the fact that the article is in a magazine and is telling location twice unnecessarily. In addition, you do not need to write "in which" and "where" in this phrase twice because they serve the same purpose- to tell where the article was put. **Choice C** is the correct answer because "in which" correctly tells where the article was and is short, introduces no grammatical errors, and does not sound eccentric.

52) This is a fragment error. There is a phrase containing background information on Houdini that needs to be set off by commas. If you look after "Houdini" you will see a comma. This is the first comma used to set off the phrase, but you need a second at the end of the phrase to complete setting it off. This question is testing if you know where to put it and if you know what word to use immediately after to let the sentence flow. Choice F and J are wrong because they contain no comma at all. Choice G is incorrect because you need to put a verb after the comma, and "being" is not a verb. **Choice H** is the right answer because it puts a comma after the last word of the phrase, "spiritualism", and uses a verb directly after.

53) What would this essay lose if we omitted the sentence about Houdini being skeptical of supernatural beings and fantasy creatures? A is wrong because the sentence has nothing to do with the friendship of Houdini and Sir Arthur Conan Doyle. The sentence contains background information on Houdini's beliefs. Choice C is also incorrect because this sentence doesn't actually state reasons for Houdini's beliefs, but tells about Houdini's beliefs. Choice D is wrong because the sentence is significant, for it talks about Houdini's interest in solving hoaxes and reveals the reason why Sir Arthur Conan Doyle probably sent the picture to him- to see if they were real or not. **Answer B** is the correct because the sentence first tells Houdini's point of view on the matter, which is negative, and then the next sentence states how Houdini thought the pictures to be false.

54) This question is testing punctuations and transitions. Choice F is incorrect because you can't have "but" and "though" in the same sentence because they both convey contrast or

opposition. G and H are also incorrect because when you use though at the beginning of the sentence, it calls for a comma at the end of the phrase because it is a dependent clause. **J is the right answer** because it contains a comma and does not repeatedly use words to show contradiction.

55) This is a rhetorical skills question. So, let's pick the least concision-challenged choice that is still legitimate. This is obviously not B because you shouldn't use "of the fact that" after "because" because you can shorten the sentence by removing this phrase. Notice that "because they had a disagreement" makes more sense and is much shorter because of the removed "of the fact that". Choice A is also incorrect because of the whole the-fact-that-they-had thing, which is even longer than the phrase above. The sentence would also make sense if you said "due to the disagreement". Choice C is wrong for pretty much the same reason as A. **D is the best answer** because it is short and gets the point across without too many words.

56) This is rhetorical skills question testing organization. We will need to make this sentence a new paragraph because at the preceding sentence is talking about a disagreement between Houdini and Conan Doyle. This next sentence is talking about Frances Griffiths, exposing her own joke. They are two totally separate thoughts and need to be separated into different paragraphs. Therefore, we can eliminate choices F and G. H is wrong because you don't say "Since some" because since is unnecessary because it's already implied that it's "since" the incident. **Choice J** is the best answer because it is not redundant and separates the thoughts into different paragraphs.

57) Choose the right pronouns to use in this sentence. Choice A is incorrect because if we took away the extra subject, her cousin, that section would read "...admitted that her had staged the photographs as a practical joke." which would not make sense. For the same reason, we can eliminate choice B because "admitted that herself had staged the photographs" does not fit either. Choice D is also wrong for the same reason as B, except the compound subject is inverted so it reads "her

cousin and her" rather than "her and her cousin". Either way, they are both wrong. **Choice C** is the right answer because if you removed either of the subjects from the compound subject, the sentence would still make sense. For example, if you removed "and her cousin", that part of the sentence would read "admitted that she had staged the photographs", whereas if you removed "she and" that part of the sentence would read "admitted that her cousin had staged the photographs".

58) This question tests your knowledge of tenses. Note that they are asking which answer would not be acceptable. There is nothing wrong with choice F, G, and J. The only wrong **answer is H** because "using" is present tense, and the sentence is in past tense.

59) Chose the option that is related best to the opening sentence of the essay. The opening has Sherlock Holmes in it, so **B would be the best answer** because it also has Sherlock Holmes in it. Choice A has nothing to do with the first sentence, Choice C talks about Houdini, who wasn't in the first sentence and choice D also has nothing to do with the first sentence.

60) This is a rhetorical skills question testing your understanding of the essay. So did the essay successfully show how belief in the supernatural affects the works of authors? No, because they didn't really talk about or give specific examples of Doyle's writings being significantly changed by his belief in mythological creatures. This renders choices F and G wrong. Choice H is also wrong because no where in the essay does it say specifically that his belief in fairies and the supernatural didn't influence his writing. The essay does not argue this at all. **Choice J** is correct because the essay keeps the topic around how one author (Doyle) responds to the possibility of supernatural beings.

61) This is a pronoun error. Choice A is wrong because "whose" would make the part of the sentence after the comma a clause, when it has to be independent to make a complete sentence. Choice B is also incorrect because the sentence is talking about "her", not "them" and the given answer choice "their" is plural, and referencing "them". Choice D is wrong for

the same reason as A. **Choice C** is the correct answer because the phrase containing "her" now has a subject to talk about, and the subject is also showing possession like the sentence requires, and is also singular.

62) This question tests punctuation. Answer G is wrong because using "and" is inappropriate. The phrase "and over one thousand letters to upwards of one hundred correspondents" needs a verb to make sense; that choice would only work if they had incorporated something like "were sent" after. Choice H is wrong because semicolons are used to break complete sentences. Choice J is wrong because "Over one thousand letters to upwards of one hundred correspondents" is a fragment. **Choice F** is correct because the original sentence uses a colon. Colons are used in front of a list or definition of the preceding word or phrase. The section after the colon is defining correspondence.

63) This question is testing rhetorical skills and punctuation. Choice A is incorrect because although a new paragraph need not be made, there should be a comma after woman. Choice C is incorrect because you don't need to make a new paragraph- the topic sentence is "Dickinson's lifetime…" and the next sentence fits perfectly, going into detail about how different periods of time had different tone of letter. Also, there is a comma inappropriately placed after "wrote". We can also eliminate choice D because you don't need to make a new paragraph. **Answer B** is correct because it doesn't start a new paragraph, and there are no punctuation errors.

64) This is an idiom error. Answer G is wrong because "to" should not be used where it is and it is unnecessary. Answer H is incorrect because it is not in the same format as the other example given- "of pinning for a valentine" does not say "of her pinning for a valentine". The "her" is unnecessary. For the same reason, Choice J is incorrect. The **correct answer is F** because it is simple and follows the same format as the preceding example.

65) This is another rhetorical skills question. Which answer tells how the letters played a role in Dickinson's life? Choice A only

talks about the time range she wrote to others, not what effect they had on her. Choice B is also incorrect because it is off topic and unrelated to the letters. Answer C is wrong because it does not tell you about how her life was affected, but only that her letters were revealed after death. **Choice D** is the best answer because it tells you how the letters affected her personally- she enjoyed hearing her friends' news and reflections on political events.

66) This is a punctuation question. F is incorrect because a semicolon breaks the sentence incorrectly, and "speaking of relatives and friends whom had died" is a fragment and cannot be put alone after a semicolon. G is also wrong because the sentence is past tense and "speak" is present tense, and it's also a run on sentence. Choice J is incorrect because "speaking of relatives and friends whom had died" is a fragment and can't be made into its own sentence. **Answer H** is correct because the comma correctly breaks the sentence and conjoins an independent clause with a dependent clause.

67) This question is testing your knowledge of who/whom. Reference the who/whom rules in the introduction. Who died? She died, not her, so you would use who. The correct **answer is B**.

68) Here's yet another punctuation question. The sentence does not need a break at all, and all the answers except for G have breaks in them, so they are all wrong. **G is the correct** answer because it has no breaks, and the sentence doesn't need them.

69) In this question, unclear pronoun reference is being tested. Answer A is incorrect because "her" does not specify that Susan is giving Emily feedback- it instead sounds like Susan is giving herself feedback. Choice B is also wrong because the "her" is placed before "Emily", which still causes confusion because since "Emily" is not placed first, so the "her" has nothing to describe. Answer D is incorrect because this choice makes no effort to solve the issue at hand- directing the pronoun to the noun it's taking the place of. The right answer is **choice C** because "Emily" is placed before "her", so the pronoun "her" has a noun to describe.

70) Here's a rhetorical skills question. For this question, you have to find the ending that is most relevant to the sentence. All of them are grammatically correct. However, all the choices are incorrect except J, because they don't have much to do with what is being talked about in the paragraph. The only logical answer from the choices **would be J** because it ends with a period, and does not add any unnecessary ending, like the other answers.

71) This is another rhetorical skills question. In this question they are asking which choice illustrates an interaction between Susan and Emily the best. Choice A is incorrect because even though Susan read the poem, this does not show any sort of interaction between her and Emily. Answer B is also wrong for the same reason as A. Susan may have liked the poem, but that doesn't show her communicating with Emily. C is incorrect for the same reason as A and B. **Answer D** is the best answer because it depicts Susan actually communicating with Emily by suggesting revisions.

72) Redundancy is being tested here. In many cases, though not all, the shortest choice is the best choice. This applies to this question. Answer G is wrong because "other" and "alternate" are synonyms, and therefore you do not need both. Choice H is also incorrect because "alternate" and "additional", in the way "additional" is being used, are synonymous. And J is also wrong because it can be inferred that the alternate versions are revised, so it is unnecessary to use both "alternate" and "revised" in the sentence. **The best answer is F** because the phrase "wrote two other" is understandable and simple and gets the point across without too much trouble.

73) Here, a couple of topics are being tested. Choice A is incorrect because "letters" and "reveals" do not agree in number- "letters" is plural and "reveals" is singular. Don't be fooled by interjecting phrases like in this sentence- the test tries to trick you here by separating a noun from its action. Answer C is wrong because the passage is past tense, not future tense, and "will" usually indicates future tense. D is incorrect because this phrase implies that what the sentence was talking about

wasn't revealed, when in fact it was revealed. **B is the best** choice because it agrees in number with letters and is present tense.

74) Choose the correct pronoun. Choice F is incorrect because "one" is just another way of saying you, and we're talking about Emily Dickinson. Answer G is also wrong because "people's" is not referring to Emily. And J is wrong because "their", once again, is not talking about Emily. **H is the best** answer because "her" is the best pronoun to use when talking about Emily, since it actually refers to her.

75) Comma usage is being tested here. Choice A is wrong because no comma is necessary after "legacy of letters", nor after "perhaps". Choice B is also incorrect because no commas are necessary after "this" and "letters". C is wrong because once again, no comma is necessary after "letters". In fact, no commas are needed whatsoever in this phrase, and **D** has none, deeming it **the correct** answer.

ACT MATH TEST EXPLANATIONS
By **Rajiv Raju**

Please refer to the questions in the Math component of the practice test in official ACT booklet, Preparing for the ACT (form 0661C).

1) When faced with word problems that involve translating dissipations to mathematical expressions, first identify the constant and variable components and be careful not to mix-up these components. The most common mix-ups will be listed as wrong answer choices. The first thing you should do is to see what is constant and what varies. In this problem, the base price, or the cost of the machine, $39.99, is the constant. The cost to make each balloon, $2.00 a piece, is the element in the equation that varies. "b" is the variable for the number of balloons. We now have everything necessary to form our expression in this case:

$$\$2.00b+\$39.99$$

This happens to be answer **choice A** on the test. This expression has the correct variable ($2.00b) and constant ($39.99) terms. Three of the wrong answers do not have a constant term. Choices B, D, and E, are wrong because they have no constant in the expression and two of the choices have random values that are not given in the problem. Choice C is wrong because the value that is supposed to be constant (39.99) is placed in front of b and is varied, while the value that is supposed to vary (2.00) is made constant.

An alternative approach to this problem involves trying easy numbers and testing the answer choices. What is the total cost to produce 3 balloons? From reading the problem we can calculate this cost to be $45.99. Testing the answer choices we see that A is the only answer that gives this value. If you choose to use this approach do not start with numbers like 0, 1 or 2 which will often work for some of the wrong answers. If the number you pick works for more than one answer choice then you have test more numbers until you can find the one correct choice. In this case if you tested b=1 it would work for both A,

C and D. Trying numbers is probably not worth the time if you can figure out how to translate the word problem to a mathematical expression. However, this approach is helpful if you are not sure how to do the problem using the usual method.

2) This problem is very simple and there is no other way to do it other than plugging in the values for the variables and following the order of operations and rules of addition and subtraction. Since this is a very simple problem, it should be very quick and the other answers are wrong because they are computation errors you can make while evaluating the values for x and y. If you were careful then you should get the correct answer 36 or **choice K**. If made an error you should identify your error so that you can try to avoid it in the future. If you picked H you probably carelessly subtracted 1 form 5 instead of adding.

3) This problem might seem very tedious at first, but there is an easier way to do it. Since the teacher taught the students 5 words on the first day and 3 words each day after that for 19 more days, we can just multiply 3 and 19 and add 5:

$(3 \times 19) + 5 = 62$

This is the number of words that the students learn in 20 days, and this happens to be **choice B**. When ever you are given these types of number problems, another way to find the answer quickly is to write out the values for the first few days and see if there is a pattern.(Remember that quote by Albert Einstine) Actually writing out some numbers will help you see the pattern. If you familiar with arithmetic series from your math classes, you may see that this question deals with that concept. However, you can still answer this question correctly even if you are not familiar with this concept by using the common sense approach.

4) This problem tests your ability to correctly use the rules of exponents to simplify the expression. When doing this problem, you should make sure to follow the rules of exponents while raising the powers of the values in the parenthesis. If you simplify correctly, you should get- $64x^6$ or **choice G**. Choice F has the correct coefficient, but a wrong exponent for x. Choice H doesn't follow the rules of

exponents, and the 4 is multiplied by3 in stead of being raised to the third power, even though the exponent on x is correct. Choice J makes this same error, and the exponent on x is incorrect, because 3 is added to 2 instead of multiplied, which is the rule when raising an exponent to a certain power. Choice K completely ignores 4 and only raises the exponent of x to the third power. When you are raising a value in parenthesis to a certain power, make sure you raise all of the terms in the parenthesis.

5) This problem asks you to find all of the positive factors of 8, which is one of the easiest problems you will come across. First you must know what a factor is. A factor is a number that multiplies into a larger number evenly. If you do not know all of the factors of 8 off the top of your head, you can try every number from 1 through 8. The obvious values are one and 8 and if the answers don't have these values, you can eliminate them, so you can eliminate B and C. If you find the other factors, they are 1, 2, 4, 8, which **happens to be E**. Answer A is wrong because it does not include 2 and 4, and answer D is wrong because 16 and 32 are not even factors, but they are multiples.

6) To do this problem, we need to combine all the like terms. Follow the order of operations to do this and multiply out the parenthesis getting:

$8x+14-6x+12$

Then you combine the x's and the integers to get $2x+26$, which is **choice H**. Answer F is wrong because it has a random x value and has 2 as the integer. This mistake can be made when you forget that the answer is positive when you multiply -3 and -4. In G, this same mistake is made even when the x value is correct. Answer J is wrong just because it has random values for x and the constant. This is also true for K.

7) This is a very easy problem. All you have to do is drop the lowest score and then take the average of the remaining numbers: 78, 83, 84, 93. The average of this 84.5 which is **answer E**. Choice B is wrong because you get that answer if you forget to drop the lowest

score. Choice A is wrong even though it drops the lowest score because it still divides the answer by 5 instead of changing it to 4 because there are only 4 values.

8) Notice that the answers are in increasing order. If we want to try out the choices to see which answer will work, the easiest way to do this problem is to start with the middle choice H and go from there, but first you have to set up equations for each cable provider. For the first one, Uptown, you try to find the terms that vary and the terms that are constant. The term that varies is the $25 a month charge and the constant is the one time $120 setup fee. For Downtown, the constant is the $60 one time set up charge and the thing that varies is the $35 a month charge. If we let x be time in months, our 2 expressions:

Cost for Uptown =25x+120

Cost for Downtown=35x+60

Now we start testing the answers with choice H. Since Uptown costs more for choice C, 10 months, we can eliminate J and K, now we try choice G. This choice happens to make the price of the two providers equal, so **choice G** ,6, is the answer. Since we have already found the answer to the problem we do not need to try F.

An alternative approach is to realize that when the costs of the two cable providers are equal the equation is true:

25x+120=35x+60

If you solve for x you get the correct answer 6.

9) Although this problem looks very tedious, it is not. The key phrase in the problem is "adjacent sides meet at right angles". This lets you conclude that opposite sides are parallel. Since the sides opposite the sides with unknown values are given, we can just assume that all of the unknown sides add up to the side opposite them. All you have to do now is calculate the perimeter as you would in a square for this particular problem. Since the sides opposite the unknown sides are both 20 each, we can conclude that the sum of the unknown vertical and horizontal sides each add up to 20. We just add them up and we

get 80 or **choice B**. This is really the only choice that can be reasonably derived from the information given.

10) The easiest way to solve this problem is to set up 2 equations:

x+y=11

x-y=5

If you add the two equations together, you get 2x=16 because the y variables cancel out. This becomes x=8, and you plug this into the first equation to get 3 for y, and you multiply these to get 24, which is **choice J**. Some possible traps are answer choices F, H, and K. In F, the answer is only the y value, not xy. In H the answer is the x value, not xy. In K the value is multiplying the difference, 5 by the sum, 11, which is completely incorrect. Wrong answers often will be numbers that you may get while doing the problem, but are not what they are asking for. Make sure that you are actually answering the question.

11) You should memorize the formulas for perfect square binomials. In this problem we would use the formula:

$$(a+b)^2 = a^2+2ab+b^2$$

If we apply this for the given expression and we get $9x^2+42x+49$, which is answer **choice E**. Choice A is wrong because it only multiplies each term in the parenthesis by 2 instead of squaring it. Choice B is wrong because although it squares x, the coefficients and constants are still only multiplied by 2. Choice C is wrong because, it does not follow the special case and forgets about the 2ab. Choice D is wrong because it only multiplies ab instead of 2ab in the expression. If you forget the formula, you can still do the problem by using FOIL on (a+b)(a+b), but you can answer the questing much faster and with less chance of error if you know the formula.

12) This is a simple problem of calculating the slope given 2 points. The formula for the slope is:

Slope= change in y / change in x:

$$slope = \frac{y_2 - y_1}{x_2 - x_1}$$

If we plug our points in to the formula we get:

$$slope = \frac{2-7}{-5-6} = \frac{5}{11}$$

This turns out to be 5/11, which is answer **choice J**. Answer choice F is wrong because it just adds the two y values. Answer choice G is wrong because it just subtracts the 2 y values. Answer H also subtracts the 2 y values only. K does not follow the rules of division and keeps – (5/11) instead of 5/11 because it disregards that 2 negatives make a positive when dividing or multiplying. If you are a calculator wiz and have a program on your calculator to calculate slope, you will not find your decimal answer in the choices and will have to figure out which answer choice corresponds to your answer. This is another example when calculator overuse can make the problem more complicated.

13) The simplest way to do this problem is to solve the equation. There are multiple ways to do this, but only one will be discussed here. First, you multiply each term by 3, to get rid of 1/3x, then 4, until you get this:

4k+3k=12

Then you combine the k terms to get: 7k = 12, then you divide and get k = 12/7, which is answer **choice B**. This is the only reasonable answer that can be derived from manipulation.

14) If you know the Pythagorean theorem, this is an extremely simple problem. For right triangles:

$$hypotenuse^2 = leg1^2 + leg2^2$$

$$hypotenuse = \sqrt{(leg1^2 + leg2^2)}$$

In our case leg1=6 and leg2=7:

$$hypotenuse = \sqrt{6^2 + 7^2} = \sqrt{85}$$

The correct answer is **choice G**.

.

The ACT often gives answers in radical and fractional form. If you had done the whole calculation on calculator without looking at the answers, you would waste time and increase chance of error by trying to figure out which answer choice matches your decimal calculator answer. Use the calculator only when you need it. On the ACT some times the calculator actually slows you down.

Choice F is wrong because it is just adding the 2 values and taking the square root of the sum. Choice H does this also except it doesn't take the square root. Choice K just multiplies the 2 side lengths, which does not help you find the hypotenuse.

15) The simplest way to do this problem is to add up the squares and the square fractions. There are 18 full squares and 4 fractional

squares. You can estimate the sum of the square fractions to be 2 full squares. Match up all of the like squares and fractions and add them all together and you get 20, or **choice C**. A potential source of error is not adding the fractions correctly or disregarding the fractions all together.

16) This question tests your knowledge of geometry. We are given enough information to conclude that triangles ADB and BCA are congruent right triangles using the HL theorem for right triangles. We are given that one leg is congruent. The hypotenuse is shared. We have to look at the answers and decide which one cannot be reasonably inferred from the given information. All of the choices except G are corresponding parts of the two congruent triangles. G cannot be determined because there are no sides or angles that can be used to determine their congruence. **G is the correct answer**. Choice F is wrong because it can be inferred because they represent corresponding parts of congruent triangles. Choice H is wrong for the same reason except these are segments of the longer sides. J is wrong because corresponding angles in congruent triangles are congruent. Choice K is wrong for the same reason.

17) For this problem we have to set up an expression to describe the situation. Since it is talking about 23%, we have to convert this to .23 for the problem. Since p is the price and 0.23p is the amount of discount. p-0.23p is the discounted price. This is **choice A**. Choice B is wrong because if forgets the p after 0.23. Choice C is wrong because it has 23 instead of 0.23. D is wrong because it does not have 0.23p or the decimal in front of 23. E is wrong because it only shows the discount, not the discounted price.

18) To do this problem we need an understanding of triangles and their angles. First, you should write down your given information in the designated areas: 76 degrees, 47 degrees, 140 degrees. Since we know that the sum 2 angles that form a line is 180 degrees, CBD is 40 degrees. Now that we have that info and 47 degrees, we find that CDB is 93 degrees. From that, we find that CDA is 87 degrees. If we add the measures CAD and CDA, we get 163 degrees. Since there are 180 degrees in a triangle, we subtract:

180-163=17, which is **answer H.**

19) To do this problem, we need to know the formula: D=RT, which is *distance equals rate times time.* First, we need to find the time it takes to drive with the given info. By plugging in 900 and 50 for D and R respectively and solving, we get T=18 hours. The problem asks how much the average speed is for this time-3, which is 15. Now we set up our equation again except now we solve for R and plug 15 hours into T. Solving, we get 60 mph. We must subtract the original speed to get the speed increase, or how much Ms. Lewis needs to increase her average speed. The answer is 10, which is **choice C**. A possible trap is choice E because that is the only the answer for the number of hours of driving, not the question. Choice D is also a trap because that is just the time it take after subtracting 3 from 18.

20) The simple way to attack this problem is to try the answer choices. First, see if all the answer choices divide evenly into both numbers. This is easy because you have a calculator. You find that G does not plug into 180x evenly, so you can eliminate that since the answers with x in them are going to be the greatest answers out of the remaining because in this question x can only be a positive integer, you can also eliminate F. Now, you just pick answer with the largest coefficient, 36x is the answer, which is answer **choice K**.

21) If you look at the table you should see that the larger bags give you the lowest cost per lemon. To get the lowest cost we want to get as many large bags as possible without going over 20. We can only get one bag of 12 and one bag of 6 without exceeding 20. 12+6=18 so we need to get two bags of one to get exactly twenty. If we add up the cost of one bag of 12, one bag of 6 and two bags of 1 you get the lowest cost to get 20 lemons which is $3.90 or **B**. Some of the other answer choices also give the cost of 20 lemons but they do not give us the lowest cost to get exactly 20.

22) This problem tests your understanding of absolute value. Since it is asking for the maximum diameter that satisfies the inequality:

$$|d-3| \le 0.001$$

Choices H, J and K satisfy the inequality but **only K** gives the maximum diameter. The other choices do not satisfy the given inequality.

23) For this problem, the easiest thing to do is to just factor the expression and see which answer corresponds to your answer. If you factor like you were thought in your math class you will get (5x+2)(x-3), which is **choice A**. All of the other choices either mix up the signs of the numbers or interchange the integers 3 and 2 in the factors. If you have trouble factoring you can try the answers until find the correct one, but factoring will be faster.

24) The easiest way to do this problem is to plug in answers and see which one will cause the answer to yield 3/5. You need to add red marbles until the probability of picking a red marble is 3/5. To start, you try out H. Because the answer is greater than 3/5, you can eliminate J and K. If you try G it is still greater than 3/5. If you **try F**, you get 18 out of 30 marbles are red, which is 3/5, which is the answer.

25) If you know the definitions of trigonometric ratios, this problem will take 5 seconds. For any acute angle θ in a right triangle:

$$\sin \theta = \frac{opposite}{hypotenuse}$$

We are told that the triangle is formed by a diagonal in a rectangle. So we can infer that the triangle is right. For angle w the opposite side is x and the hypotenuse is y. Since all the answer choices have the ratio (x/y) in them, we know the answer has to have sin in it because opposite/hypotenuse(x/y) is equal to sine. The only **answer choice** in it with sine **is D**. All other choices are wrong because they show incorrect rules for all the other trig ratios. Even if you have not had a course in trigonometry is worth memorizing the trigonometric ratios since they are tested on every ACT test.

26) When you given an equation for a line in the y=mx+b form the slope is m. We are given two equations in this form. Therefore, if the slope is larger, the "m" is larger. So if the first equation has more slope, then a>c is the only possible answer, which is **answer J**.

27) There are six nails. From any nail you can stretch five rubber bands to the other nails. If you did this at each nail you would have placed 5 x 6 = 30 rubber bands, but you would have placed two rubber bands between each pair of nails. The total number of ways to stretch one rubber band all the nails is half this number which is 15 or **choice A**.

Another way to approach the problem is to draw all the possible lines and count them. If you try this approach you have to have an organized way to draw all lines without duplication.

28) To do this problem, add up all the participants to get 280. Divide the number of runners aged 26-35 the total to get 112/280 to get 0.4. Now you just multiply .4 by 60 to get your answer, 24, or **choice H**. This is the simplest way to do it, although you could set up a proportion:

112/280=x/60

and then solve for x. This would take a little more time to solve, however, and your aim is to take the least time possible on each question while still remaining accurate.

29)   To do this problem, all you have to do is apply the given formula for the volume of the cylinder to find the volume of water. Remember you were asked to find the volume of water, not the pool. We have to use a height of 5 ft   First, you interpret the given information to find your radius, 12 ft, and your height, 5 ft.

$$volume = \pi r^2 h = \pi 12^2 5 = 2262$$

When you use this formula you get volume of 2262 which is the answer, rounded to the nearest cubic foot. This happens to be **choice C**. Be sure not to waste your time on unnecessary information, like the degree measure, 75, that is given in the problem. This is irrelevant to finding the volume of the cylinder.

30) This problem requires you to find the circumference of the pool, and then solve the rest of the problem from there. The formula for circumference of a circle with radius r is:

$$circumference = 2\pi r = 2\pi 12 = 24\pi = 75.4$$

Using an r of 12 we get a circumference of 75.4. Since you are given the degree measure of the arc, you just divide that measure by the total degree measure of a circle to find the fraction of the circle that makes up the arc:

45/360= 0.125

After this, you can multiply that fraction (or decimal) by the circumference of the pool to find the measure of the outer arc: 9 .425.

0.125 x 75.4 = 9.425

But that is not the whole problem. You must also add the radius, which is 12 feet. If you add these two values, you get 21.425.

9.425+ 12 = 21.425

This is closest to 22 in the answer choices, which **happens to be G**. Some potential errors are finding the area instead of the circumference, or not adding the radius length after finding the outer arc length.

31) To do this problem, you need to know how to translate this problem into a graph representing it. Since the pool is increasing the whole time, and the rate of increase slows after the larger flow hose stops, the graph will decrease in slope at a certain point after the beginning. The only graph that represents this is **graph E**. Graph A is wrong because it shows a smaller slope then a larger slope. Graph B is wrong because it has a decreasing graph. Graph C is wrong because it is constantly increasing. Graph D is wrong because it is also decreasing.

32) To solve this problem, you need to set up an equation with the trigonometric ratio for tangent. For an acute angle θ in a right triangle:

$$\tan \theta = \frac{opposite}{adjacent}$$

For this problem x is the unknown adjacent side we are trying to determine:

$$\tan 75 = \frac{6}{x}$$

Solving for x:

$$x = \frac{6}{\tan 75}$$

which is answer **choice F**. A possible trap is J because it messes up the ratio by using adjacent/ opposite, resulting in x/6=tan 75, which yields 6 tan 75.

33) This problem is very easy because all you have to do is set it up. Plug in the variables and you have the answer. If you plug in 5%, you get 5/100, which is .05. Plug in 782,000 for P_o and 10 years(2000-1990) and you get $782,000(1.05)^{10}$, which is **choice C**.

Be careful not to be tricked by other answers. For example, E puts 782000 into the parenthesis, when it is supposed to be kept outside, as stated in the formula.

34) To do this problem, you should first go down the chart and group each call into its respective pricing and then go from there. Then you should multiply the prices by the number of minutes in each part of the chart and add all the charges up. If you do your addition correctly, you should get $8.80, which **is choice J**. Be sure not to get the PM times mixed up with the 7:00 pm-7:00 am .10 cent period.

35) For this problem, you have to use the properties of trapezoids and the Pythagorean theorem to solve the problem. First, since the trapezoid is and isosceles trapezoid, you can draw heights on either side of the smaller parallel side inside the trapezoid. Since the smaller side is 10 and the larger side is 16, and this is an isosceles trapezoid, you can divide the remaining length 6 in half, giving you one of your sides in a right triangle. Since the hypotenuse is 5, and the known side of the triangle is 3, the other leg must be 4. This is also the height and answer **choice B**. The ACT often uses Pythagorean triples. This is a 3,4,5 triple. Knowing these Pythagorean triples increases your speed and accuracy.

36) This is a very straight-forward problem. All you have to do is solve for x in the inequality.

$3(x+2) > 4(x-3)$

$3x+6 > 4x-12$

$x > 18$

First, you have to distribute out the expressions on each side of the inequality. There are many ways you can manipulate this problem, but the quickest is to move the 3x to the right and the -12 to the left, resulting in:

$18>x$, or in proper terms, $x<18$

This is answer **choice K**. If you don't mess up the manipulations and follow all the steps just as you would a normal equation with the few exceptions in inequalities, this is one of the easiest problems you will encounter on this test.

37) For this problem, you need to have an understanding of the midpoint formula.

Given two points (x_1, y_1) and (x_2, y_2) the midpoint (x_m, y_m) is:

$$x_m = \frac{x_1 + x_2}{2} = \frac{1+x}{2} = 4$$

$$y_m = \frac{y_1 + y_2}{2} = \frac{-5+y}{2} = -3$$

Using this formula we get 4=(1+x)/2 and -3=(-5+y)/2. Solving for x we get x=7. Solving for y we get y=-1. x+y=6 or **C**.

38) To do this problem, you need to know how to factor out terms from an expression. It is worth memorizing the difference of squares formula:

$a^2-b^2=(a-b)(a+b)$

$$\frac{x+1}{x(x^2-1)} = \frac{x+1}{x(x+1)(x-1)} = \frac{1}{x(x-1)} = \frac{1}{x^2-x}$$

If you look at the denominator of the expression, you can factor out an x right at front you are then left with $x(x^2-1)$.   You can further factor this expression (easy of you realize that you are dealing with a difference of squares) to get the following value in the denominator:

x(x+1)(x-1)

There is x+1 in the numerator, you can cancel out the x+1 to get x(x-1), which turns into x^2-x, with 1 in the numerator.   The final answer should look like **choice J**.

Beware of trick answers like H, which has a -1 in the denominator instead of –x.

39) You can determine angle ACB is 50 degrees because 180-130=50 since a straight line forms 180 degree and we are given the other part of the straight angle is 130. Because the sum of the angles of a triangle is 180 we can determine that angel ABC is also 50.You then proceed to fill in all the angles that are congruent to 50. If you follow these rules of congruence for vertical angles, corresponding and alternate interior angles of the transversal of parallel lines, you should find 8 angles that are congruent to 50 degrees, which is **choice C**.

40) To solve this problem, you first need to set up an equation representing the adult and student tickets and how much they all add up to.

3x+2y=600

is the equation, with x representing the adult tickets, and y representing the student tickets.   The coefficients represent their prices respectively.

If you isolate y, you get:

y= -(3/2)x+300

Since the y intercept is 300, we can eliminate all answers besides K and H. If you find the slope of each line, you find that **H** is the only one with $-(3/2)$ as the slope. Beware not to pick the answers that have 600 as the y intercept, such as F and G. This occurs if you forget to divide the entire expression by 2 when you have 2y=-3x+600 and leave 600.

41)This is perhaps the easiest problem you can ever encounter on this test. All you need is knowledge of the elementary concept of median. This problem is made even easier because there are seven numbers. All you have to do is order them in increasing order and pick the one that is right in the middle, or the 4th number. This number is 42, which is answer **choice A**. A trick answer is choice E. Although 79 is the 4th number, this series of numbers is not ordered correctly.

42) This problem is just a factoring problem with the addition of absolute value signs. If you factor the expression: $|x|^2+2|x|-3$, you get $(|x|+3)(|x|-1)$, which leads to: $|x|=-3$ and $|x|=1$, which in turn leads to $(+$ or $-)1$ and $(+$ or $-)3$, which would appear to be the answer. But for absolute value problems, you always need to check your final answers, and if you plug all your answers in you find that $+$ or -1 are the only answers that work. **The answer is F**. Choice G is the opposite of the right answer, and only can occur if you check your answers wrong. Choice H is wrong because not only does it disregard the absolute value, it contains an answer that doesn't fit. Choice J also makes this error. If find factoring with absolute value confusing, just try all the answers until you find the correct one.

43)To do this problem, you need to have an understanding of the slope formula(change y/change x). Since you are given (2,5), you can see what y value you have to subtract to get 2, and this is 3. Since the only answers with 3 as the y value are A and D, you can eliminate all other answers. Now you see which value leads to -3(since the final answer is negative), and this is 5. The only answer with these x and y values **is D**, (5,3).

44) In this figure, we are given 2 right triangles. Since we are given a 30 degree angle in one triangle and a 60 degree angle in the other,

we know these are the special 30, 60, 90 degree triangles. This establishes that the triangles are similar, and that corresponding sides will be in proportion. The long legs will be in proportion. The only ratio that is correct is **choice F**, or AB: AD. Choice G is wrong because it is comparing one of the legs of the smaller triangle to the hypotenuse of the larger triangle. H is wrong because it doesn't even compare sides of the separate triangles, but only sides in the larger triangle. Choice J is wrong because it compares the wrong legs instead of the corresponding legs. Choice K is wrong because it also compares one of the legs of the smaller triangle to the hypotenuse of the larger triangle.

45) To do this problem, you first need to know that the triangle formed is an isosceles triangle since it is extended from 2 sides in a regular pentagon, where all the sides are congruent. You now have to find the measure of all the angles in the polygon, and we can use the formula for the sum of all interior angles and divide by 5 to get the measure of one angle:

sum of interior angles of polygon of n sides=(n-2)x180

for a regular pentagon each angle is

((5-2)x180) / 5=108 ....you plug in 5 for n in the formula.

If you do this you find that the pentagon has a measure of 108 degrees for each of its angles. Now you can find the measure of the angles of the triangle, which are the same because the triangle is isosceles. The measure for both base angles is 180-108=72. Now you can find the measure of x by adding 72 and 72 together and subtracting from 180, getting 36, or **choice C**. Choice E and D are both traps. Choice E is a trap because it answers the wrong question, the measure of the base angles instead of the measure of x. Choice D is something you would get if you tried to estimate with your eyes, because it resembles a 45 degree angle.

46) To do this problem, you must NOT confuse surface area with volume. You need to know that a cube has 6 faces. From there, you just find the area of each face, 9, because the edges are 3, and multiply by 6, the number of faces, which gives you 54, **or K**. Choice H is a blatant trap because it gives the answer for volume and not surface area. Choice A is also a trap because it has the area of a square with edge 3, not a cube with edge 3.

47) This problem is very easy, but it is easy to get tricked. The easiest way to do this problem is to start with 100. You increase 100 by 25%, giving you 125. You then take 20% away from 125 you get 100 again, which happens to be **choice C**. Do not fall for choice D which incorrectly subtracts the percentages to get 105%. For these percent increase and decrease problems it is helpful to assume that you are dealing with the number 100.

48) For this problem, you need to use the definition of reciprocals. Just plug in a number for x to see which choice corresponds to that number's location on the number line. Let's try 2 for this problem. The reciprocal of 2 is ½ since 2x1/2 is 1. This is **choice J**, which states that the reciprocal is between 0 and 1. Remember that a number's reciprocal is just a fraction with the number in the denominator and 1 in the numerator. (3 the reciprocal is 1/3). Choice F is wrong because a number that is greater than 1 times its reciprocal cannot be negative. Choice G is wrong because in this choice, the answer is still negative. Choice H is wrong because the reciprocal cannot be 0 because you cannot have a real reciprocal that is 0 since 1/0 is undefined. Choice K is wrong because the reciprocal of a number greater than 1 cannot be also greater than 1. The reciprocal of this type of number is always a fraction.

49) This is a very straight-forward problem. You might be thrown off by the awkward presentation of the inequalities(-1>x instead of x<-1). Since the graph is greater from 3 onwards or is less than or equal to 1, the correct inequality **is D**. A is wrong because it says that x is greater than or equal to 1, when it is less than or equal to 1. C is wrong because in makes the same mistake in A and also mixes up the second part by saying that x is less than or equal to 3. Choice E is wrong because it states that x is less than or equal to 1 , but wrongly states that x is less than or equal to 3.

50) This problem is easy if you know how to translate the word problem into an equation. The problem seems complicated since it asks for a graph that for each y coordinate, it is 1 less than the square of the x coordinate. You can translate this into an equation, however:

$y=x^2-1$

Now this is just a simple translation problem where you have to identify the graph. Since the -1 is not in parenthesis, that means there is a vertical shift 1 unit down from the standard graph of x^2, a parabola. The only choice that has this **is J**. Choice F and G are wrong because they are not even parabolas. Choice H is wrong because it makes a vertical shift 1 unit upwards instead of 1 unit down. Choice K is wrong because it flips the graph over the x axis and shifts it down 1 unit, giving it the graph of: $y=-x^2-1$.

51) To be able to do this question you have to understand that they are asking for the smallest number that can be repeatedly divided evenly by 3 4 times. . Easiest way to do the problem is to try the answer choices on the calculator. Only one of the answer choices can be divided evenly by 3 repeatedly 4 times. 81/3=27, 27/3=9, 9/3=3 and 3/3=1. The correct answer is **81 or E**. If you start with the middle choice 27 or C you can save time by not having to try all of the choices. 27/3=9 and 9/3=3 and 3/1=1 so we know that 27 is too small and we do not have to try the smaller choices A and B. Now try 54 54/3=18, 18/3=6,6/3=2 but 2 is not divisible by 3 so the answer must be 81 or choice E.

52) To do this problem, you have to just plug in numbers to find which rule it satisfies. For this, it is very important to check for multiple numbers! Let's use 1 and 2. If we look at F We can see that m is odd, but if you use 2 and 3, you see this rule doesn't hold up. Choice G also is true for some cases with consecutive integers, but not when n is even. Choice H is wrong for all cases since the difference of consecutive integers is always 1. **Choice J** is the only choice that works for multiple possibilities of consecutive integers. n^2-m^2 is odd is always true for all consecutive integers. Since you have found your answer, there is no need to check K. For these types of problems, it is always good to start with the first choice and go down.

53) While this problem may seem complicated , this problem just asks you to follow the rules and evaluate the expression. Since the number you are evaluating for is less than 0, you use the second function. If you plug it in you get P(-1)=-70, or answer **choice A**. Be sure to follow the rules. A common misconception for piecewise functions is that you plug in the variable for both functions and add them. You MUST pick the function that satisfies the number being evaluated.

54) This problem tests your understanding of the formulas regarding a circle. The diameter, 3 feet, is given, and 5 inches must hang over. To do this problem, the first step must be to add the entire length of the diameter including the extra 5 inches on each side. 3 feet is 36 inches. You add 10 inches to that since the diameter is the distance between 2 sides going through the middle of the circle. This adds up to 46 inches. However, if you look at the problem, 46 inches is not an answer choice. But the problem asks which choice is the minimum needed, and **48, or K**, is the only choice that satisfies the need for 46 inches. Although these types of problems may stump you, you must always remember to read the question carefully, not missing any key points.

55) This question tests your understanding of the basic graphs of sine and cosine. However, this problem is very easy if you have had trigonometry. If you have not had trigonometry you need to learn that a_1 and a_2 determine the amplitude. Just order the graphs up in increasing amplitude. Obviously, 0 has an amplitude of 0, a_2 has the smaller visible amplitude, and a_1 has the larger visible amplitude. The answer that orders these correctly **is B**. Don't get confused by these graphs. Comparing the amplitudes is the easiest way to order the graphs with the highest values.

56) You have to know the pathogen identity to do this problem:

$$(\sin x)^2 + (\cos x)^2 = 1$$

Solve this for sin x and cos x to get:

$$\sin x = \sqrt{1 - (\cos x)^2}$$

$$\cos x = \sqrt{1 - (\sin x)^2}$$

If you substitute the above expressions into the expression in the problem you get:

$$\frac{\sqrt{1-(\cos x)^2}}{\sin x} + \frac{\sqrt{1-(\sin x)^2}}{\cos x} = \frac{\sin x}{\sin x} + \frac{\cos x}{\cos x} = 1 + 1 = 2$$

This is answer **choice H**.

57) To do this problem, you need to understand function notation and how to combine functions. You are given a point (4, 6) and 2 functions that the point passes through: $f(x)=\sqrt{x}$ and $g(x)=7x+b$. You are asked to find $f(g(x))$. To do this, you must evaluate $f(x)$ with $g(x)$. When you do this you get $f(x)=\sqrt{7x+b}$. You now plug in the point values and simplify to get 36=28+b. Solve for b and you get choice 8, or **A**. Be careful to plug the point values in the end of the problem.

58) This problem tests your knowledge of reflections and where the corresponding points are reflected. The easiest way to do this problem is to draw a rough sketch of the reflection. The reflection is of x, y, and z. In the new quadrilateral, the perimeter sides are y and z. It is easy to see that the perimeter is 2y+2z, or 2(y+z), which is **choice K**. This problem is very easy, but make sure that you are reflecting across the right line, YZ.

59)This problem tests your understanding of the shape of a function graph that is odd. However, the problem is leading you to do the problem the long way, plugging in x values to see if f(-x)=-f(x). One very important concept that you should know is that odd functions, along with having the above rule, are also symmetric across the x axis. The only graph that displays this characteristic **is E**, the graph of the cubic.

60) This problem is just testing your understanding of logarithmic notation. You have to take this problem by steps. The first part is condensing the expression Log_2 24-log_2 3 which becomes log_2 8. This equals 3. Do not try to look at the whole equation including log_5 x. Once you know that the first part equals 3, you can easily solve the equation: $\log_5 x = 3$, which is 5^3 or 125, or **answer J**.

Notes

ACT READING EXPLANATIONS
By **Rajiv Raju**

Please refer to the questions in the Reading component of the practice test in official ACT booklet, Preparing for the ACT (form 0661C).

1) This question is directly asking you to state the main idea of the paragraph. When you think of the main idea of this passage, think about themes that are relevant throughout the majority of the passage. The relationship between the Eugene and the narrator is the most prevalent theme. Choice C and D can be eliminated because, while the neighbors were mentioned, they were only talked about in the introductory paragraph and referred to in the last sentence. Since A and B are both about Eugene and the girl, you must identify which one provides the most valid statement about the passage. While choice A states correctly that the narrator had trouble starting the relationship, it is evident that the two "hit it off" quite quickly and didn't have trouble maintaining the relationship because of their mutual love for books. Therefore, **choice B** is the correct answer because it says that the passage concerns the process of making a new friend, which the narrator does, and also concerns the change that the narrator makes about thinking about the present more than the future.

2) For this question, you need to read through the answer choices and see which one is the valid statement based off the information in the passage. Choice F is wrong because it is evident that the narrator has never walked in Eugene's house in the last paragraph because she says she would like to one day. Choice G is wrong because it is clearly stated in the passage that both the narrator and Eugene like books. Choice H is wrong because it is stated in the first paragraph that Eugene's house was the only house on the block with a front yard and trees. **Choice J** is the correct answer

because in the second to last paragraph, the narrator only states that she wishes to become a teacher.

3) This, like most questions on the reading section of the ACT, is an information question, or a question that gives you statements and asks you to pick the valid one based off the information in the passage. Choice A is wrong because it is evident that the old couple weren't socially out going and spent most of their time together. Choice B is wrong because, while the father has tended the lawn, the flowers are no longer there, as indicated in the second paragraph. Choice D there is no comparison made between the employment of the old couple and Eugene's parents because we don't know if the old couple had jobs or not. **Choice C** is correct because it is stated in the passage that the old couple spent a lot of time together, evident by how they cared for each when they were sick, while Eugene's dad didn't even come home for dinner.

4) In this question you need to read the given lines(67-87) and interpret their purpose. After reading the lines and looking at all the answer choices, you see that they all deal with one thing: the family of the narrator, so you need to eliminate some choices that are irrelevant to the passage or are not the primary reason that the narrator wrote the lines. Choice G is one of these because no contrast is made between her parents and the couple because the parent's feelings towards each other aren't mentioned. Choice H is wrong because it is neither stated in the lines nor the passage that the narrator's friendship with Eugene has affected her family. Choice J is wrong because it is not stated in the passage that her parent's aspirations have changed over time, and we are to assume that her parents still wanted to live on a beach in Puerto Rico one day. **Choice F** is the correct answer because it is directly stated in the passage that the narrator's perspective based on her family had changed when she met Eugene, and she now thought of her future with him.

5) This question is also asking you to look at some given lines (30-31) and pick the valid choice. Choice A is wrong because it is not stated in the passage that the flowers were still growing, so you can't assume that. Choice B is wrong

because it is never stated in the passage that the narrator watered the plants of old woman.   Choice D is incorrect because it was not stated in the passage that the "weeds intertwined with the flowers.   **Choice C** is correct because it is reasonable to infer the flowers were cut down because Eugene's father spent a few days mowing the lawn to clear it out, and it was stated that only the grass remained.

6) This question is also asking you to pick the valid answer based off of the passage.   Choice F is incorrect because it is explicitly stated in the passage that Eugene had spent time with the narrator on her fire escape before school started. Choice G is incorrect because Eugene did not seek out the narrator, rather, the narrator went out of her way to look for Eugene at school.   Choice H is incorrect because it can be inferred that when Eugene noticed narrator, he was shy and because of this he didn't introduce himself.   **Choice J** is correct because Eugene was shy around the narrator because he was nervous about reaching out, and he did notice her at school.

7) This question asks you to look at given lines(80-81) and pick the answer that provides the best explanation of those lines. Choice B is wrong because changing her opinion of her career path doesn't have anything to do with thinking more about the present than the future.   Choice C is incorrect because it is not specifically stated in the passage that the narrator wanted to return to the island, though her parents did.   Choice D is wrong because the narrators parents are unable or don't want to just go on a vacation to Puerto Rico, but rather buy a house there.   **Choice A** is correct because it is stated in the passage that the narrator looked towards the future at her employment, but then her new friendship diverted her attention.

8) This question asks you to basically paraphrase the second to last paragraph of the passage.   Choice F is wrong because the dream of living in Puerto Rico is not said to have been close.   Choice G is wrong because it is a direct contradiction to what is stated in the passage as the other people in the building do have similar goals.   Choice J is wrong because it

is not stated in the passage specifically; rather, the narrator would rather go to college become a teacher than move back to Puerto Rico. **Choice H** correctly captures the essence of the last two paragraphs and is the correct answer.

9) This question asks you to answer a question based on information alluded to in the passage. Choice A is a direct contradiction to information given in the passage because the narrator said specifically that she could not hear the neighbors. Choice B is wrong because, although the author wished to tend the flowers. Choice C is only partially valid because, while the narrator could see the couple, she could not see them in the entire house. **Choice D** is the correct answer because the only time the narrator saw the couple during mealtimes in the kitchen in the description in the first paragraph.

10) This question asks you to paraphrase one of the paragraphs dealing with her feelings towards spying on Eugene. Choice F is wrong because the narrator, while she feels "joy" of a sort by spying on Eugene, she feels dishonest rather than suspicious. Choice H is correct because there is nothing in that paragraph of the passage that indicates that the narrator felt betrayed by spying on Eugene. Choice J is incorrect because while the narrator found it pleasurable to spy on Eugene, she did not feel less of him after she met him. **Choice G** is the correct answer because the narrator felt enjoyment when spying on Eugene, yet felt guilt and dishonesty when doing it as well.

11) This question is basically asking about the overall passage since the whole passage is about Eleanor Roosevelt and what she was like. Choice A is wrong because, although Eleanor Roosevelt was socially controversial, she was not quietly cooperative and it is even stated that she disagreed with her husband openly. Choice C is wrong because Eleanor was morally strong, but she contradicted traditions and "courted radicals". Choice D is incorrect because it is a contradiction to what is stated in the passage. Eleanor was far from moderate even though she was personally driven and she welcomed radical ideas. **Choice B** is correct because ER was politically courageous by openly arguing

with FDR and was socially concerned, especially with racial and gender discrimination.

12) This question asks you to pick which choice is accurately stated in the passage regarding the question. Choice G is wrong because it is not stated in the passage that ER gave political roles for women, even if she might have done so. Choice H is wrong because it is not stated in the passage that ER was alone in her "struggle" for social reform. Choice J is wrong because not once is there any mention of "powerful White House networks". **Choice F** is correct because it can be inferred that ER brought unpopular views to the forefront of politics especially in her fight against racial inequality.

13) This question is also testing your ability to pick that choice with the information that is NOT supported in the passage. Be careful to not get confused by finding the information that is supported by the passage, and waste precious time. Choice A, B, and C are all wrong because they are mentioned in the same paragraph as what every person should have. **Choice D** is correct because it is direct contradiction to information in the passage. It is stated that ER disliked involved(complex) theories and wanted effective action.

14) This question is testing your overall understanding of the passage because you really need to read the whole passage to understand ERs approach to social reform. Choice F is wrong because although ER was passionate about reform, it is specifically stated that she does not like theoretical reform. Choice G is incorrect because ER wanted action now and she was firm in her beliefs, so this is a direct contradiction to information given in the passage. Choice H is wrong because there is no evidence in the passage to say that ERs reforms were simplistic and she changed her views on isolationism soon after the FDR took office. **Choice J** is correct because it is stated in the passage that ERs approach was progressive because it was often controversial or defied traditions and that she was determined to make these reforms occur and used her roles as first lady to its fullest degree.

15) This question asks you to pick the answer choice that is directly supported by the passage. Choice A is a direct contradiction to information in the passage because it is stated that until ER came to the White House, the people weren't committed to social reform. Choice B is wrong because it is not stated in the passage that the nation was in a time of prosperity; in fact, the nation was in the middle of a massive depression at the time! Choice C is wrong because it is a direct contradiction to information presented in the passage. Democracy was not spreading overseas; rather, communism and fascism was gaining popularity. **Choice D** is correct because it can be inferred from the information that before ER gained influence, people did not pressure the government to take care of the poor.

16) This question requires you to find the answer choice that restates the last paragraph. Choice F is wrong because it is not stated in the last paragraph that ER played "the game" only when she knew when she could win. In fact, it is stated that ER played "the game", win or lose. Choice H is wrong because it is not stated that ER placed her self in the position of president. Choice J is wrong because while it may be true, which it probably isn't, it is not mentioned in the last paragraph. **Choice G** is correct because it correctly restates the last paragraph and even includes key words that were present in the paragraph such as "agitators" and also states that she pursued justice in victory and defeat, which is also mentioned in this paragraph.

17) This question is asking you to pick the choice that makes the most sense as related to paragraph 3. Choice B is wrong because it is contradictory to information in paragraph 3. ER owned a school and co-owned a crafts factory. Choice C is wrong because there is no evidence in paragraph 3 on which you can come to the conclusion that ER had conflicting interests during her first year as first lady. Choice D is wrong because it can be reasonably inferred that the leadership positions described in paragraph 3 would prepare ER for life as first lady. **Choice A** is correct because it states that ERs successes in personal endeavors prepared her for her role because they were also leadership positions.

18) For this question, you need to understand the passage as a whole because it asks you to pick the answer that is best supported by the passage. Choice G is wrong because it is contradictory to information given in the passage because ER often brought up progressive and controversial topics as first lady. Choice H is wrong because it is not stated in the passage that ER had any personal columns or radio broadcasts. Choice J is wrong because, while one of ERs principles was to lead a bloodless American revolution, it wasn't her primary principle. Rather, her primary principle was **Choice F**, or that every person should have a dignified and decent life. This is explicitly stated in the 7th paragraph.

19) For this question you need to look at the 8th paragraph for what ER thought the relationship between the people and the government should be. Choice A can be eliminated because it is a direct contradiction to ERs ideal of the unified citizens. Choice B is incorrect because ER believed that the citizens should step up and form their relationship with the White House with out the government's assistance. Choice D is incorrect because it is not stated in the passage that radio broadcasts and formal channels should be used to control the relationship between the White House and the citizens. **Choice C** is correct because it accurately states ER believed that *community,* or unified citizen, action was required for social reform.

20) This question asks you to put the given phrase in different terms while still keeping the same meaning in the context of the passage. Choice F is wrong because it is not stated in the passage that ER's adventure was individualist. Choice G is wrong because it is also not stated that ER was a team player over a leader; in fact, it can be inferred that ER liked to take the lead through her extensive use of her first lady powers. Choice J is wrong because it is not stated that ER didn't take criticism or politics very seriously. **Choice H** is correct because it is evident throughout ER's life that she loved politics, but often received and accepted criticism on her often controversial positions.

21) You need to read the whole passage and understand its layout to answer this question. Choice B is wrong because from reading the passage, it cannot be reasonably concluded that the author tried to show that the claims she made in the first paragraph are wrong; in fact, the whole passage seems to be supporting that claim. Choice C is wrong because not once are the narrator's parents mentioned in the passage. Choice D is incorrect because for one thing, the event is probably not recent since the narrator was five when it happened and five-year olds can't write essays under most circumstances☺. Also it can be inferred that the lesson the narrator learned was very significant because it has apparently changed her entire view on life. **Choice A** is correct because the passage starts out with an assertion supported by a personal story. The story is used to show why the author has such an opinion on the topic mentioned in the first paragraph.

22) Look at the lines that are referred to(9-44) and analyze them. It is evident that the narrator is portraying a scared character that comes to a conclusion eventually. Since the question asks about mood, you have to pick a choice that would most likely be true under the given circumstances. Choice F is wrong because while the narrator has a steadily increasing amount of tension, it is not present during the whole anecdote. Choice G is wrong because it can be inferred that the narrator has a slowly increasing amount of tension as the shadow travels across her room. Choice J is wrong because there does not appear to be any elements of irony or humor in the excerpt. **Choice H** is correct because it supports the fact that the narrator has a growing feeling of tension, but that tension is dissipated when she finds out that the source of the "thing" is a passing car.

23) This question asks you to interpret the meaning of the third paragraph. Choice A is wrong because the narrator does not describe the nature of the object as much as the actions that the object is performing. Choice B is wrong because the narrator didn't do anything and all she did was observe the thing. Choice D is incorrect because the narrator does not speculate where the object came from. She is just observing its movements with detail. **Choice C** is correct because it

accurately states what the narrator is doing: observing the thing and describing its doings with lots of detail.

24) For this question, you need to find the paragraph with the required information(paragraph 2). It is evident that the narrator didn't want to wake her sister when the thing came in because she was too scared to move. You have to pick the choice that most closely resembles this inference. Choice F is wrong because the narrator hadn't even talked to Amy at all. Choice G is a direct contradiction to information in the paragraph because the narrator explicitly states that she cannot muster the charmed innocence of her sister. Choice H is wrong because it is not states that the narrator's sister Amy knew what the thing was. **Choice J** is the answer because it supports the claim that the narrator was scared because if the narrator was scared, she wouldn't want to attract the attention of the thing that was scaring her.

25) This is yet another question where you must identify the feeling of the narrator when a certain thing happened. Choice A is far from correct because if anything, the narrator would be relieved to find out what caused the thing that was causing her fears. Choice B is wrong because of the same reason: she wouldn't be unhappy if she found out the cause of the thing that is causing her tension. Choice C is wrong because it is evident that there is more that is gained than the narrator's ability to sleep at night because the rest of the essay is about how her outlook on life changed after this incident. **Choice D** is the right answer because the rest of the essay is pretty much about the insights on life that the narrator received from this conclusion.

26) This question is asking you to interpret what the metaphor referred to means in terms of the narrator coming to her conclusion. Choice F is wrong because there is no mention of monsters in the passage and this "fear" does not pertain to the metaphor given. Choice H is incorrect because although the metaphor has to deal with the boundary between inner and outer lives. Choice J is a contradiction to information in the passage because there was no bitterness when the narrator came to her conclusion and she was not leaving

comforting memories. **Choice G** is correct because the conclusion she made about the "thing" was the time when the narrator crossed the boundary between the inner and outer world.

27) To answer this question, you need to understand the theme of the whole passage: The narrator comes to a conclusion and crosses the threshold between the interior world and fantasy, to the outside world and reality. Choice A is wrong because a story that the narrator has read has nothing to do with the given phrase, which most reasonably refers to the "thing" that the narrator saw in her childhood. Choice B is wrong because of the same reason as above. Choice C is wrong because it is evident that the show of light that the narrator describes is contradictory to the outer world; rather, it is an element of the interior world. **Choice D** is correct because the show of light is most nearly a fantasy created by the mind, when really it is just a shadow of something in the outside world (the car, as the narrator found out).

28) The lines referred to (3-5), may seem hard to comprehend, but by reading them you should get the idea of what type of thought it is. Choice G is wrong because while the "self" (interior life) is mentioned many times in this excerpt, it is not referring to self examination. Choice H is wrong because the lines are focused on the "self", not analysis of nature. Choice J is wrong because it cannot be reasonably inferred that the "interior life" has debates with it self. **Choice F** is the correct answer because the lines mention how all the happenings revolve around the "self" and that these occurrences are deceptive. The words "blinds it and deafens it" relate to deceptive self-absorption.

29) This question is asking you to, like stated, paraphrase the given lines (5-8). Choice A is wrong because the lines do not state that the imagination lacks value, but it should be used in constructive ways. Choice B is wrong because lines 5-8 focus on the imagination, not reason. Choice D is incorrect for the same reason, and the words enrich is used in the wrong context. **Choice C** is correct because it accurately states, just like in the passage, that imagination shouldn't be used without focus on the real world, at least at some times.

30) This question is also asking you to paraphrase the given lines (77-80). The narrator is stating in the lines that she is relatively unimportant part of the world, considering how big it is. Choice F is wrong because, while the lines refer to how she as a child was unimportant, the lines do not say that adults are considered more important than children. Choice H is wrong because while it is stated that people could see or ignore the narrator, it is not stated whether it matters to her or not which one the people who pass her choose to do. Choice J is wrong because she is not saying in those lines that she is less valuable than anyone. **Choice G** is correct because it accurately paraphrases the lines by saying she is a part of a very large world, along with many other people and things.

31) For this question you need to have a clear understanding of the passage to see which of the conclusions presented is valid. Choice A is wrong because there is no evidence in the passage to make the conclusion that important new theories will be accepted, no matter what. In fact, that seems contradictory to the passage because it seems new theories often have slim chances of survival, especially from new scientists. Choice C is wrong because it is evident from the passage that research into new theories is not respected in the scientific community, and it is even stated that Louis Frank's theory had opposition of 10000:1. Choice D is wrong because it is specifically stated in the passage that even scientists don't want to deal with new discoveries or theories. **Choice B** is the correct answer because it is explicitly stated in the last sentence of the passage that if Louis Frank was a scientist of a lesser standing, his theory wouldn't have been taken seriously. In other words, scientists of higher standings have a better chance of successfully introducing new and unusual ideas.

32) This question asks about feelings within a certain part of the passage, specifically the opinions of Frank's colleagues after he presented his comet idea. The main thing to understand is that Franks colleagues didn't think less of him after he presented his idea, and it is stated at the beginning of the

third paragraph that his presentation probably only helped his career. Therefore, you can eliminate F and G because they say that the colleagues had lesser opinions of Frank and Sigwarth after they presented their theory, which is not true. The information in choice H is not supported in the passage, as nothing is said about Frank's colleagues thinking of him as someone who worked hard on his theory. **Choice J** is the correct answer because although the colleagues didn't take well to the new theory because they thought it was improbable, but that his research proved that there was definitely something bombarding the earth on terms with Frank's comet theory.

33) This is another question asking about the feelings of someone in the passage. It is important to note that Frank did not feel happy or proud after he presented his theory. You can eliminate C and D because of this because in C, it states that he was proud and in D it states that he was satisfied. Choice A is wrong because there is no evidence in the passage that states that Frank was treated badly after his presentation. **Choice B** is correct because it is evident that his coworkers no longer ridicule him because his research has shown there is something on par with the thing in Frank's theory that is bombarding the earth.

34) This question is asking what is implied by paragraph 4. The quickest way to answer this question is to read the excerpt and go through the answer choices to see which one best describes what the excerpt is saying. Choice F is wrong because there is no part before this paragraph where the author criticizes other scientists. Choice G is incorrect because it cannot be reasonably inferred that the author was making any statement about the scientists' role in society. Rather, he is most nearly stating that scientists do not like change as much as the rest of the laymen. **Choice H** is correct, however, because it states this exactly by saying scientists "loath to embrace radically new ideas". Even though you have found the answer that is surely correct, you should ALWAYS look at all of the answer choices regardless. By looking at Choice J, we can be sure it is wrong because it in this paragraph there is no mention or comparison of theoretical and practical scientific research.

35) This question is asking you to find specific information in the passage, yet it does not give you a paragraph to at which to look. Therefore, you should look at the first sentence of each paragraph starting with the second paragraph (the first paragraph is the introduction) until you find the information that you need. This happens to be the sixth paragraph. Choice B can be eliminated immediately because water entering the atmosphere is not even mentioned in this paragraph. The rest of the answer choices, however, are information contained in the paragraph. While the information in Choices C and D, the static on the transmissions and the specks on the satellite images, caught the scientists attention during their research, the original project was about electrical activity, or the charged particles named plasmas, accompanying sunspots. **Choice A** is the correct answer.

36) This question asks you how a certain set of lines affects the argument presented in the paragraph. Choice F sounds like the correct answer because numbers are indeed provided earlier in the paragraph and the sentence stating that the planet is billions of years old supports the statement that the water level grows an inch every 10,000 years. However, you always need to look at the other choices no matter how correct the answer choice sounds. In this case, as it is in most cases, the other choices are wrong, but that is not always the case. Choice G is incorrect because it is not implied that the evidence given had limitations. Choice H is incorrect because it can be inferred that the main purpose of the paragraph and the specific lines is not to provide additional details about how big the comets are, even though those details are provided. Choice J is incorrect because, again, the purpose of the paragraph is not to give readers the sense of how old the planet is, even though it is stated that the planet is billions of years old. So **Choice F** is the correct answer.

37) This question asks you what the scientific community most nearly thought about the comet theory. Choice A is incorrect because it is implied that although scientists were skeptical, they did acknowledge that something was bombarding the atmosphere. Choice B is incorrect because it is stated that

the scientists who were responsible for the comet theory were outvoted 10000:1. Choice C sounds correct because it can be inferred that the scientists did not agree fully with all the aspects of the small-comet theory, but that they were willing to consider that something was hitting the atmosphere on a regular basis. Again, we must look at Choice D to make sure that it isn't right. Choice D turns out to be incorrect because most scientists did NOT think that the comet theory was completely correct, but they were willing to consider it as a possibility. So **choice C** is the correct answer.

38) This question is asking you to analyze the given word and its sentence and answer in what context the word is used. Choice F is wrong because it is evident that the scientists agreed that something was hitting the atmosphere on par with the comet theory, regardless of whether it was comets or not. Choice G sounds correct because it can be inferred that although the scientists agreed that something was hitting the earth based on the information in the small-comet theory, they still weren't absolutely sure what was hitting the earth. Checking on the other answer choices, Choice H is wrong nothing is mentioned or can be inferred in the sentence about the practical value of the theory. Choice J is completely wrong because the methods that the Frank and Sigwarth use to collect evidence have nothing to do with the question whatsoever. **Choice G** is the correct answer.

39) This question asks you to rephrase what Richard Zare is saying. This is an example of a question where it is imperative that you read all of the choices. Choice A is wrong because although the term schizophrenic is used as a descriptive term, it is not meant literally. Choice B and C both sound right because they are contained in the excerpt of the passage. However, **Choice D** is the correct answer because it states that scientists have to maintain a balance of questioning and accepting current ideas. Choice B and C are both wrong because they are examples of what all scientists try to avoid being, according to Zare.

40) The question asks you to pick the answer choice that best supports the information given in the passage regarding the scientists' attitude towards their theory. The information is

perfectly stated in one sentence at the beginning of the seventh paragraph. ("After a while their curiosity…grew into a preoccupation, then bordered on obsession.") Looking at the choices, the answer that best restates this sentence is **Choice H** because it is evident that the scientists became more and more captivated by the theory to which they could find no explanation.

ACT SCIENCE EXPLANATIONS
By **Rajiv Raju**

Please refer to the questions in the Science component of the practice test in official ACT booklet, Preparing for the ACT (form 0661C).

Passage 1

1) For this problem, you actually have to look in the passage to find the answer, specifically to find the time required to replicate a gene, which happens to be 15 minutes. Since the question is asking how many complete genes can be replicated within 50 minutes, all you have to do is some simple math to find that 3 genes can be replicated in 45 minutes. Note that although there is time left, there is not enough time to replicate another full gene so the only correct **answer is B**.

2) For this problem again you have to look at the reading under Student 3. According to this theory, the replication process moves clockwise. The problem is giving you an example of this, starting with G, and you have to find the THIRD replication. If you follow the directions, this is easy and you should get Gene X, or **choice J**. Be careful however, not to pick the consecutive gene just when you figure out how to do the problem.

3) You have to look at the reading yet again for this problem. The question is asking which of the students supports the idea posed by the question, which is, that replication can start with any gene. Luckily, it turns out that the answer for this question is in the first sentence of every paragraph for the students. Using this insight, you can quickly eliminate A and B because those students' theories postulate that the replication can only start with specific genes. While D has the correct answers, it also contains Student 2, which is wrong. Therefore, **C** is the correct answer, which is Student 3 and Student 4.

4) For this problem, you need to understand two key pieces of information from the passage: the replication process takes 15 minutes and that replication in student A's theory starts with X and ends with F. The problem asks which gene will not be replicated if the process is interrupted after 45 minutes following the constraints of Student A's hypothesis. Since 3 genes are replicated after X, the only gene that is not replicated is Gene G, which is answer **choice F**. Be careful not to start with gene F and from there, as the information from student A can be easily misunderstood.

5) This question is asking the same question as problem #4 except it is asking about student 2 and tells that the replication is interrupted after 30 minutes. By following the instructions of student 2 and starting with either X or F(then replicating 2 genes), we can see that neither gene A or gene S is replicated. However, only A is in the answer choices, so the answer is **A**.

6) This problem is quite easy if you realize that this problem is problem 3 reworded. Since it is asking which students would agree that replication would end with gene A, all you need to do is look back and see that students 1 and 2 say that the replication ends with specific genes, which are either F or X. Only 3 and 4 say that replication can begin and end with any gene. Therefore, the answer is **J**.

7) By adhering to the constraints set by student 1, you start with gene X and move one gene, 15 minutes at a time until you get past gene A. This means 4 genes(X,R,S,A) have been replicated. 4 times 15 minutes is 60 minutes so the answer for this straightforward problem is **D**.

Passage 2

8) For this question, you simply need to find the graph that corresponds to study 1 and interpret the graph. You can cross out H and J because the S allotrope is increasing only. Out of choice F and G, you need to look at SO_2's graph. The graph increases at first, but then decreases. **Choice G** is the

only choice that gives this description of SO_2's graph and the correct description for S's graph

9) For this question you have to look at the corresponding graph for study 3. The question is very simple since there are only two pieces of data that you need to look at. From looking at the graph it is very easy to see that large plumes always give off a reflectance that is less than of smaller plumes. It never has greater reflectance than the smaller plumes. **Choice C** is the answer to this question.

10) For this question you need to carefully read the correct curve on the correct graph and estimate a value from the graph. Find the corresponding graph for study one and look at .40 on the wavelength axis. See at what value of reflectance that white S passes over this wavelength. The reflectance is about .2, which is **choice H**.

11) For this question you look at the graph for the Pele crater floor in study 2. You need to compare these similar graphs to one of the allotrope graphs from study 1. The Brown S graph is the closest to the graph of Pele, and this is **choice D**.

12) This question is asking you to do some simple linear extrapolation, or extending of the graph. Since .61 is very close to the end of the graph on the x axis, .60, you should find the answer choice with the closest reflectance values to those at .60 uM, Large: aprox. 0.5 Small: aprox. 0.9. Therefore, **choice H** is the answer.

13) For this question, you need to look at the graph corresponding to study 1 and the definition of reflectance, which is the fraction of light that strikes a surface that is reflected by that surface. This pertains to a specific wavelength. Choice A is wrong because it only accounts for the 2% that is LEFT. Choice C is wrong because it accounts only for the 2% left and it says that it reflects all visible light when reflectance only pertains to a specific wavelength. Choice D is also wrong because of this. **Choice B** is the only correct answer

because it has the correct wavelength and the correct
percentage of reflectance: 98%

Passage 3

14) For this problem you need to look at the corresponding graph
for experiment 1. The question asks you what the time
constant is for a value that is not present on the chart.
Fortunately, they are not asking for a specific number, which
makes this question much easier. Find where 7.6 Volts would
be, which is between 0.0 and 8.4. For the voltage to be 7.6,
the time must be less than 12 seconds, which is **choice F**. All
the other choices are wrong because they list the time
constants for voltages greater than 7.6.

15) For this problem you need to look at table 2. The question
asks you to do some extrapolation with the data given. It
asks you to find the time it would take to reach across a 6 volt
capacitor for a given capacitance, whose value is on the chart.
The question asks for 1.5x10^-6, when the data on the chart
only goes up to 1.2x10^-6. Immediately you can eliminate
choices A and B because they are less time than 1.2x10^-6.
There is a .3 increase between 1.2 and 1.5. If you notice on
the chart, there is a .3 increase in capacitance between .3 and
.6, and the time increase is 2.1. There for, for every .3x10^-6
increase in capacitance, there is a 2.1 second time increase.
You can add this time to 8.3 seconds and get 10.4. The
closest answer to this is answer **choice C**, 10.5 sec.

16) This question is simply asking for the two variables in the chart
in experiment 3, which is one of the easiest questions you will
encounter on the science section of the ACT. On the chart
there is resistance and the time to reach 6 V across the
capacitor. If you look through the choices, the only choice
with both of these variables is **choice J**.

17) This question just requires a little common sense. Since they
are asking which circuit would only measure the voltage
across the resistor, you should look for the choice where the
line labeled "V", or the voltmeter, only goes around the
resistor. According to figure 1, the resistor is the squiggly line
at the bottom of the circuit. If you look at **choice A**, the line

labeled V is only surrounding the squiggly line, which is the resistor, so this is the answer.

18) This question is asking which set of values for capacitance and resistance will cause the least time for the voltage to change. If you look at the table for experiment 2 and 3, you see that as both capacitance and resistance increase, the time required for the voltage to travel increases. So picking the lowest values for both of these will yield the least time. **Choice F** is the correct answer because out of all the answer choices, it gives the lowest values for BOTH capacitance and resistance. While choice G may have the same value of capacitance, it has a higher value of resistance, and vice versa for choice H. Choice J is the completely opposite answer for this question, as it gives the highest values.

19) This question is basically asking what is the relationship you found between capacitance and time you found in question 18. As capacitance increases, time increases. The hypothesis presented in 19 is true, so you can eliminate choices C and D. In choices A and B, however, there is a trick. The choices are essentially giving the same information, but choice A is listing the wrong experiment. Capacitance was not tested in experiment 1, but only in experiment 2. **Choice B** gives the accurate information and the correct experiment, so it is the correct answer.

Passage 4

20) In this problem, they tell you the tables of which to refer. You need to see the overall relationship present by the two charts. First, on table 2, you see that if you increase the amount of sucrose, the amount of heat released increases. These two charts may not seem alike at all, but you need the information in both to answer the question. You use table 1 to relate the heat released to the change in water temperature. The information is not in successive order, so do not be tricked into picking H just because that is how the information appears on table 1. If you match up the heat released and the change in water temperature and put it in successive order, you see that

as the amount of heat released increases, the change in water temperature also increases and only increases. This is **choice F**.

21) This problem is asking you to represent the answer to the previous question in a graph. Because you found that as the amount of heat released increases, the change in water temperature increases, you should find a graph that has a constant positive slope since a direct proportion that is increasing has a consistently positive slope. Choice A is incorrect because while it is increasing, the graph levels off at a certain point. Choice C is incorrect because it shows the graph having a negative slope. Choice D is incorrect because it shows the graph level at first and then having a negative slope after a certain point. **Choice B** is the correct answer because it is a line with a positive slope that is always increasing.

22) This question asks you to evaluate the relationship between the two variables on table 2: the amount of sucrose and the heat released, and asks what happens to the amount of heat released if the amount of sucrose is halved. Since the upper four values (.5 to 4.0) of sucrose are in increments on twice the previous value, it is easy to see this relationship. If the amount of sucrose is halved, then the heat released is approximately halved as well. Choice A is wrong because it is the opposite of what would happen if the amount of sucrose was decreased. Choice H is wrong because ¼ is not the value by which the heat released is decreased. Though choice J correctly states that the amount of heat released would decrease, it does not give the correct factor of decrease (1/2). **Choice G** is the correct answer because it says that the amount of heat released would decrease and it gives the correct factor of decrease.

23) This question is asking you to put in order the foods relative to their amounts of heat released considering 1 gram of food. By looking at table 1, since all the foods are shown in 1 gram, it is easy to put them in order of heat released. However, you must also account for sucrose, which is in table 2. In table 2, you must find the value of heat released for 1 gram of substance, which is 16.0 kJ. By putting these all in order, you

get: Potato, Egg, Bread, Sucrose, and Cheese. This is answer **choice A**.

24) For this problem you don't specifically need the information given in table 2, but you need to use it to realize that the amount of heat released relative to a food sample added is a linear proportion. Table 2 indicates a linear proportion with the property that as the amount of sucrose doubles, the amount of heat released doubles as well.   If you look at table 1, you see that the mass of potato is 1 gram. The question asks for the heat released for 5.0 grams of potato. All you have to do is multiply the amount of heat released for 1 gram of potato, 3.2 kJ, by 5, which is 16.0 kJ. Of the answer choices, this value is closest to choice H, 15 kJ, so the answer is **H**.

Passage 5

25) This question is asking you to analyze the graph in figure 1. However, the question is also asking you what happens when the temperature *decreases* from 10 to 0 degrees. This means that you need to interpret the graph backwards. Following the graph backwards, you see that it is increasing until about 4 degrees, but then starts decreasing until it reaches 0(degree symbol needed for these numbers). **Choice D** is the correct answer because it accurately states this. Choice A is wrong because the graph does not just increase because it reaches a peak and then decreases. Choice B is wrong because that answer would be interpreting the graph in the wrong direction because at first the graph is increasing. Choice C is wrong because it is the exact opposite of what the graph does, which is increase, then decrease.

26) For this problem, you need to compare the densities of solids and liquids in table 1. Since the hypothesis tells you that every solid compared to every liquid is greater in density, you must find the liquid with the greatest density and compare it with the densities of the solids. Mercury is the densest liquid in the chart, with a density of 13.59 g/cm^3. You can see that its density is greater than any solid on the table because the

greatest density, Lead, is only 11.34 g/cm³. You can get rid of H and J because the hypothesis is wrong. Choice F states the hypothesis is correct, but says that lead has a density greater than any liquid, which is a direct contradiction to the information presented on the table. **Choice G** is the correct answer because it gives an accurate statement and states the hypothesis is wrong.

27) This problem requires you to make a very simple interpretation of the linear graph in figure 2. It asks you what happens as temperature increases, and it is easy to see that the graph decreases as temperature increases because of the negative slope. Therefore, the answer to this simple question is **B**, because the graph only decreases. Choice A is the exact opposite of the graph, and choices C and D describe a graph that is not linear.

28)   For this question, you need to know that lower density substances are higher up in a solution.   This is one of the rare cases where you need to have prior knowledge for the science reasoning test. If you look on the table with the densities, you see that ethyl ether has a density of .71 and that mercury has a density of 13.59.   From the information given in the question you find that water has a density of .9971.   From this information and the rule that lower densities are higher up in a solution, the correct solution would have: ethyl ether first, water second, and mercury third.   This is **choice F**.

29) This question is very easy, but very easy to be tricked in as well.   First, you need to find the density of water at 4 degrees Celsius, which is 1.000 g/cm³.   However, the question asks you the density when there is 100 grams of water. Now all you have to do is some simple multiplication, because 1 x 100 is 100, obviously.   The answer is **C**. Don't be tricked by finding the density for only 1 gram of water, which is choice A. Choice B and D cannot be reasonably derived from the information given.

Passage 6

30) For this question, you need to look at the graph corresponding to study 4.   By looking at the graph key, you can see that the

line with squares going through it denotes frugigroves. If you look at the graph, the line for frugivores is steadily decreasing. **Choice F** is the correct answer because it correctly states this correlation. Choice G and H are wrong because the graph is consistently going downwards; it does not change its relative correlation to change the sign of the slope.

31) For this question, to need to look at figure 3 evaluate each answer choice to see if it contains valid information based off of the graph. It is safe to assume that the number of captures is directly proportional to the populations of the animals Choice A is wrong because, while the population of hummingbirds is increasing, the population of insectivores is decreasing drastically. Choice B is wrong because the population of hummingbirds increased. Choice C is wrong because it is the exact opposite of the information presented in the graph: the population of insectivores did not increase, it decreased and the population of hummingbirds did not decrease, it increased. **Choice D** is correct because it accurately states that the population of insectivores decreased and that the population of hummingbirds increased.

32) For this problem, you need to look at figure 1, the graph for study 1, and do some linear interpolation with the given value of 75 meters to find the change in AGTB. Since 75 meters is between 70 and 80 meters on the graph, you can see that the change would be about less than -2 but greater than -3. The only value in the answer choices that fits in these restrictions is -2.6, or **choice G**. Be careful not to pick choice J because the values for the change in AGTB are negative.

33) For this problem, you need to see which choice is a reasonable explanation for the constant AGTB. Choice A and B can be eliminated because increasing or decreasing the AGTB would obviously not yield a constant average AGTB. **Choice C** is correct because increasing and decreasing the AGTB at the same time can keep the average AGTB constant. Choice D is wrong because the study was conducted in the forest and increasing the AGTB would not yield a constant AGTB. It is easy to see that many ACT questions just require a little common sense.

34) This is one of the few questions where you have to do some reading of the passage(excluding the conflicting scientists passages). You need to look at the thesis, which is generally in the introductory paragraph, to find the prediction of the researchers. You need to look at the slope of the graphs to answer this question. Since the researcher's hypothesis is supported by data in studies 1 and 2, you can eliminate choices F and G. Choice H is wrong because the graph for frugivores validates the hypothesis that animal populations would decrease with fragmentation. **Choice J** is the correct answer because it is least consistent with the hypothesis because the population of hummingbirds is increasing, when the hypothesis states that the population of animals would decrease with fragmentation.

35) This problem is very simple, but it is easy to be tricked. They are asking how many insectivores would be trapped if 10, 000 hours were spent every year trapping birds. The graph in study 4 is in units of 1,000 hours per year. First you need to find the amount of insectivores trapped in year two for 1,000 of trapping, which is 80 insectivores, and multiply that value by 10 to see how many would be caught with 10,000 hours of work. This would be 800 insectivores, or **choice C.** Choice A is the trick because that is the answer that is presented on the graph. However, as stated before, the graph is in units of 1,000 hours of trapping per year.

Passage 7

36) For this question you need to look at the information given and compare it to the information given on the figures to find the best answer. A good place to start is matching up all the pieces of information on one chart. If you look at Table 1, you see that gray C is the closest to the percent volumes of sand, silt, and clay, with 31.7, 33.6, and 34.7 respectively. While the closest answer appears to be Gray C, you must look at figure 1 to make sure. Sure enough, the resistivity of gray till C is a little less that 100, which is close to 85 ohms, and the CO_2 content is a little above 20 mL/g, so the answer is **choice H.**

37) For this question, you need to do some reading of the introductory paragraph. From reading this, you find that it is indirectly alluding to the fact that older glaciers are lower underground. This should also be common sense for most people and can be considered one of the few things that they must know for this test. With this information, it is easy to say that **choice D**, or Gray till D, is the answer because it is the deepest glacier.

38) For this question you need to look at the resistivity part of figure 1 and compare the resistivity graph of sand and gravel to that of the till layers. It is easy to see that sand and gravel has a higher resistance than any of the till layers, so the answer is **choice G**. Choice F is wrong because it is the complete opposite of the information presented in the graph, which states that sand and gravel had the highest resistivity. Choice H is wrong because it is not supported in the figure at all as no two sections have the same resistivity. Choice H is wrong because sand and gravel's resistivity is considerably higher than that of bedrock.

39) The simplest way to do this problem is to draw a line from the approximate end of the bedrock graph and see in which section it has the closest intersection. If you do this, you find that olive green and gray till have resistivities most liked bedrock. Therefore, answer is **choice C.**

40) This question asks you to look at Figure 1 and at the CO_2 data. Since the question tells you that data was collected at a site where the CO_2 content was much greater than any till, all you have to do is look for the area where CO_2 reaches its highest point. This is between 30 and 40 on the graph or approximately 35. Therefore, you need to find an answer choice greater than 35 mL/g, and the only answer choice that satisfies this **Choice J,** greater than 35 mL/g.

Notes

www.ingramcontent.com/pod-product-compliance
Lightning Source LLC
Chambersburg PA
CBHW070554030426
42337CB00016B/2491